Etching of The Pheasantry as it was in the early 1900's by the author.

The Pheasantry, The Untold Story.

ISBN - 1- 913218-66-9

THE PHEASANTRY

THE UNTOLD STORY

The Pheasantry c. 1937

Contents

The Pheasantry c. 1964

Introduction

'The Pheasantry' : what a profanely insipid name for this perverted palace, which might be a chapel of Beelzebub, Aleister Crowley's pied-à-terre, a crèche for Rosemary's baby or a finishing school for vampires'.

Bevis Hillier, 1969

The Pheasantry has had a rich and colourful history that has remained largely untold. Some claim its name came from its past as a pheasant farm, where birds were reared for the Royal household. Others say it was built for Charles II's lover, Nell Gwynn. Neither are true, but The Pheasantry has no need for fictions. The true stories and secrets its walls hold are as vivid and wonderful as any that could be invented. Though we will see that invention and deceit form a large part of its history.

This book is a biography in pictures; the images tell a remarkable story of this historic building. The documents I have gathered; pictures, letters, cuttings and autobiographical recollections are as close as we can get to asking the walls to reveal the many secrets they have held for more than two hundred and fifty years.

I discovered The Pheasantry as a singer, performing in its recent incarnation as Pizza Express' cabaret venue, which replaced the old Pizza on the Park ten years ago. I was immediately curious. Where did it gets its name? What was behind the bizarre French-style façade with the words on the brickwork: 'Amadée Joubert and Sons, Upholderers…' How had I missed the crazy arch on the King's Road that takes you into the courtyard? And who was Princess Astafieva commemorated by the English Heritage blue plaque?

I wanted to find the answers to these questions and it spurred me to look deeper into The Pheasantry's past. I was soon piecing together parts of this untold history; unearthing countless accounts and photographs from its many incarnations: as menagerie, members club, studios and forge, and haven to lovers, artists and crooks.

Joanna Strand

October 2019

Detail from engraving of "Common Peacock. Ringed Pheasant. Horned Pheasant. Silver Pheasant" engraved by J.Bishop after a picture by J.Stewart, published in *A History of the Earth and Animated Nature*, 1865. Steel engraved print with original hand colouring, 1865.

The Beginning

A 'ring-tailed monkey', or lemur, just like Jocko, who lived at Baker's Pheasantry in 1865.

Steel engraving published by William Mackenzie, Glasgow, 1860.

Baker's Pheasantry

ARC DU CARROUSEL.

In 1865 Samuel Baker moved his Pheasantry from Half Moon Passage to 152 King's Road, where he would be visited by royal princes and maharajahs.

Following a trip to Paris, he erected a grand entrance arch topped with a horse drawn chariot in the style of the Arc du Carousel.

The Pheasantry sold much more than pheasants; it was more of a menagerie with ring- tailed monkeys, 'Angola cats', horses, guinea pigs and all sorts of fantastic birds on display. Baker won prizes for his Breton cows. Popular at the time because of their diminutive size, they were known at the time as the 'lady's cow' or 'house cow'.

FIGURE 1   Bretonne cow, drawn after Harrison Weir's picture in J Coleman, *The Cattle of Britain*, 1875.

Illustration from The Agricultural History Review:'Breton Breed of Cattle' in Britain, C.M. Baker/ C. Manwell, 1889.

BY SPECIAL APPOINTMENT TO THE QUEEN & H.R.H. PRINCE ALBERT.

BAKERS PHEASANTRY,

AND

BEAUFORT STREET, KINGS ROAD, CHELSEA,   HALF MOON PASSAGE GRACECHURCH STREET.

Samual Baker

The inhabitants of Chelsea are under deep obligations to Mr. Baker, for erecting one of the most interesting spots, by far, in the parish, and which has already, before it was entirely finished attracted the attention of Royalty. To call it 'The Pheasantry' seems almost a misnomer, though there are beautiful specimens from various countries including the gold and silver penciled pheasants, for it is more like a zoological gardens, on a small scale, the variety of objects being so numerous…

May 20th 1865 Middlesex Advertiser

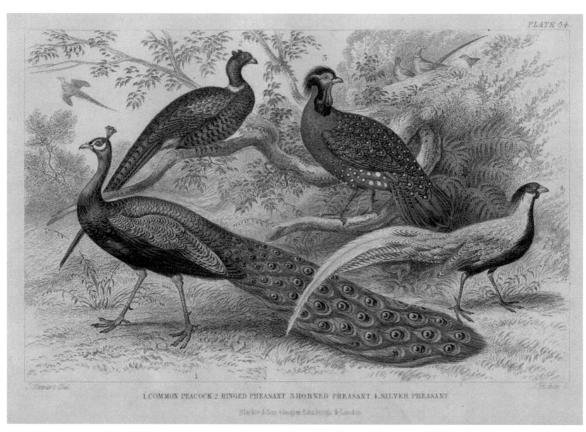

Detail from engraving of "Common Peacock. Ringed Pheasant. Horned Pheasant. Silver Pheasant" engraved by J.Bishop after a picture by J.Stewart, published in *A History of the Earth and Animated Nature*, 1865. Steel engraved print with original hand colouring1865.

The Pheasantry- Many of the residents in Eaton and Belgrave Squares, or at least those who have but recently take up their abode there may not be aware they have such a treat in their immediate neighbourhood as Mr Baker's Pheasantry, in the King's- Road. Pheasantry is misnomer, for, although there are gold and silver pencilled pheasants from all lands , yet, there are Mandarin, pintailed, and all sorts of ducks, and geese from all climes, and swans, black and white, and fowls of all descriptions and monkeys, and Angola cats, and small birds of every description, from the zebra paraquet, to the laughing jackass of Australia, and horned owls, with eyes as big as tea saucers, and Shetland bulls and cows and ponies, and we do not think these are all included in the order Phasianus Colchicus.

West Middlesex Advertiser, June 30 1866.

The Maharajah's calling card, © Courtesy Autograph ABP

THE MAHARAJAH DHULEEP SINGH. — The Maharajah honored the Messrs. Bakers with a visit of two hours duration, at the Royal Pheasantry, King's Road, Chelsea, yesterday, September the 7th, 1865.

Middlesex Advertiser September 8, 1865.

One of the first royal visits to The Pheasantry was by The Maharajah Duleep Singh, at its opening in 1865. The Maharajah Singh was the last Sikh ruler of the Punjab and following his brief reign, he was exiled to Britain. Here he became close to the Royal family, spending summers with them at Osbourne House on the Isle of Wight. Queen Victoria called him her 'beautiful boy'.

The Royal Princes visiting cards from 1865 and 1866

In 1865, a 25 year old Prince Edward VII visited The Pheasantry with his younger brother, Alfred.

THE PRINCE OF WALES VISIT TO CHELSEA.— H.R.H. The Prince of Wales, accompanied by H.R.H. Prince Alfred, honoured Messrs. Baker's, new pheasantry, 152, King's-road, Chelsea, with a visit, to view the different varieties of foreign pheasants, previous to their being penned for the season, as well as the large collection of ornamental water fowls, foreign birds, &c., from which H.R. Highness made some selections.

STEREOSCOPIC Cº.   Copyright.

THE PHEASANTRY.

The inhabitants of Chelsea are under deep obligations to Mr. Baker, for erecting one of the most interesting spots, by far, in the parish, and which has already, before it was entirely finished, attracted the attention of Royalty. To call it "the Pheasantry," seems almost a misnomer, though there are beautiful specimens from various countries, including the gold and silver pencilled Pheasants, for it is more like the Zoological Gardens on a small scale, the variety of objects being so numerous. Shetland Ponies, the smallest in the world. A bull, and cows of the same breed. Fowls of various descriptions, feather-legged Bantams, Spanish, spangled Poland, black Poland, with large white top-knots, Cochin China, &c., &c., and large horned Owls, with eyes so brilliant and splendid, that no lady in the land has their equals! And poor little Jocko, the ring tailed Monkey, and Swans, and Geese, and Ducks, from every clime, including some beautiful specimens of the Mandarin Drake, Angola Cats, Pigeons, the Piping Crow, Zebra, Paroquets, &c., &c. It is indeed an exceedingly interesting spot.

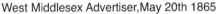
West Middlesex Advertiser, May 20th 1865

Charles Darwin's letters and account books show he bought numerous species (alive and dead), including a number of 'Laughing Jackasses' (kookaburras) and guinea pigs, which he used for his experiments and writes about in his research.

THE GUINEA-PIG.——*Cavia Cobaya.*

The Wellcome Collection. R. Clay printer.

Joubert, Amédée and Son

STEMMA JOUBERT.

Felix Joubert arranges for a forge to be delivered to The Pheasantry via the Joubert Studios entrance on Jubilee Place. Opposite page: a room in The Pheasantry, courtesy Mike Bell.

The Jouberts took over The Pheasantry in 1880, when they gave the building its new, French style facade, on which they announced their business to the residents of Chelsea:

'Upholsterers, painters, decorators, furniture makers, gilders, stained glass makers, fresco painters, theatrical designs and scenery, manufacturers of French bedding, importers of oriental carpets and Lyon silks…'

They were patronised by royalty, making and copying a vast array of products. Each room of the building was decorated in a different style to show off the products on offer.

The Joubert family business employed numerous artists and craftsmen to execute their commissions. Many of these artists and artisans lived in The Pheasantry, and later in Joubert Mansions, which was built on the land belonging to The Pheasantry, on Jubilee Place.

In 1895, they built Joubert Studios just behind the Pheasantry, which could be accessed through the main house, or by an entrance on Jubilee place. But it was in 1897 that the young Felix Joubert added to the family's real estate portfolio with an extraordinary addition.

A corner of La Tourelle, Chelsea, where the armour has been housed during the thirty years in which Mr. Felix Joubert has collected his specimens.

Above: One of Joubert's Turret House gargoyles, and detail of exterior, courtesy of Kensington and Chelsea Library.
Below: the interior room of Turret House or La Tourelle as Joubert called it, which housed his considerable collection of arms and armour, before he donated it to the City of Nice in 1926, where it was displayed in Musée Masséna. Picture from The Graphic - Saturday 20 February 1926

Turret House, 12 Jubilee Place

Felix Joubert designed and built himself Turret House at 12 Jubilee Place. The house was like a miniature French chateau, complete with gargoyles and turret, and was connected to The Pheasantry by a secret passageway. His addition to the Pheasantry estate tells us a lot about the most eccentric member of the Joubert family.

The Egerton Coopers in Turret House, photographs by Brain Wharton for Harpers 1969.

By the time Felix Joubert inherited the family business he was living in Turret house with his wife, Blanche. Many years later in 1969, Bevis Hillier visited The Egerton Coopers in Turret House and describes the interior as:

'a glorious melange if the interiors of Cheverny, Chenonceaux, Charmont, Chambord and Azay- le-Rideau... Felix carved the caryatids above the main fireplace when he was only seventeen... Felix was also a European fencing champion, and I was shown the large corner cupboard where he kept his épées in a nest of red plush'.

Bevis Hiller, Harpers 1969

Felix Joubert...

Fencer

Felix Joubert was not only an artist, architect, interior designer, arms and armour expert and forger, he was also a European prize winning fencer.

And if as if that isn't enough, he was also a film producer. 'Field of Honour' was based on a famous medieval battle and allowed Joubert to indulge his considerable knowledge of weapons and warfare. Some of the scenes were shot at The Pheasantry. By the time he made the film, he had built The Chelsea Picture Playhouse (1910), and the film's premiere was held there in 1922.

Both Felix and Blanche starred in the film, alongside the famous English actor, Percy Moran. The cast also included famous boxers of the day, and thousands of Belgian troops, whom the Belgian government placed at Joubert's disposal. There are no surviving copies of the film.

Opposite: Joubert's 'A Proclamation' states clearly his enthusiasm for film as moving image in which through 'marvellous alchemy whereby animated pictures are to be shown on a screen'. Pictures courtesy M. Bell.

Filmmaker

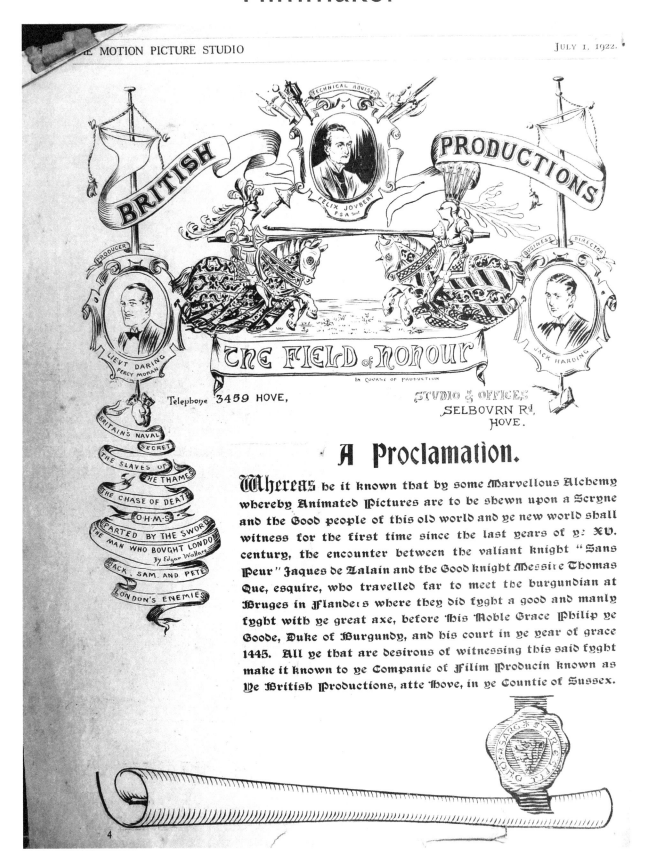

BRITISH PRODUCTIONS

TECHNICAL ADVISER

FELIX JOUBERT
F.S.A. Scot

PRODUCER

LIEVT DARING
PERCY MORAN

BUSINESS DIRECTOR

JACK HARDING

THE FIELD of HONOUR

IN COURSE OF PRODUCTION

BRITAIN'S NAVAL SECRET
THE SLAVES OF THE THAMES
THE CHASE OF DEATH
O·H·M·S
PARTED BY THE SWORD
THE MAN WHO BOVGHT LONDON
By Edgar Wallace
JACK, SAM, AND PETE
LONDON'S ENEMIES

Telephone 3459 HOVE,

STVDIO & OFFICES
SELBOVRN Rd,
HOVE.

A Proclamation.

Whereas be it known that by some Marvellous Alchemy whereby Animated Pictures are to be shewn upon a Scryne and the Good people of this old world and ye new world shall witness for the first time since the last years of ye XV. century, the encounter between the valiant knight "Sans Peur" Jaques de Lalain and the Good knight Messire Thomas Que, esquire, who travelled far to meet the burgundian at Bruges in Flanders where they did fyght a good and manly fyght with ye great axe, before His Noble Grace Philip ye Goode, Duke of Burgundy, and his court in ye year of grace 1445. All ye that are desirous of witnessing this said fyght make it known to ye Companie of Filim Producin known as Ye British Productions, atte Hove, in ye Countie of Sussex.

4

25

Architect: Joubert's Electric Cinema

The Electric Cinema Theatre, next to The Pheasantry art 148 King's Road photographer unknown

Some years after Joubert showed his film in his own cinema, the Chelsea Picture Palace was taken over by Classic Cinemas (1937). It was one of the first cinemas to specialise in showing classic Hollywood films. But in August 1973, the cinema screened its final double bill, 'Little Caesar' and 'Bullets or Ballots'.

From August until October 1973 the building had one final burst of life before closing, when the original stage show of 'The Rocky Horror Show', transferred here from The Royal Court's Upstairs Theatre where it became an immediate hit.

After the short run of The Rocky Horror Show, The Classic was demolished, and today the building that took its place is a branch of Boots the Chemist.

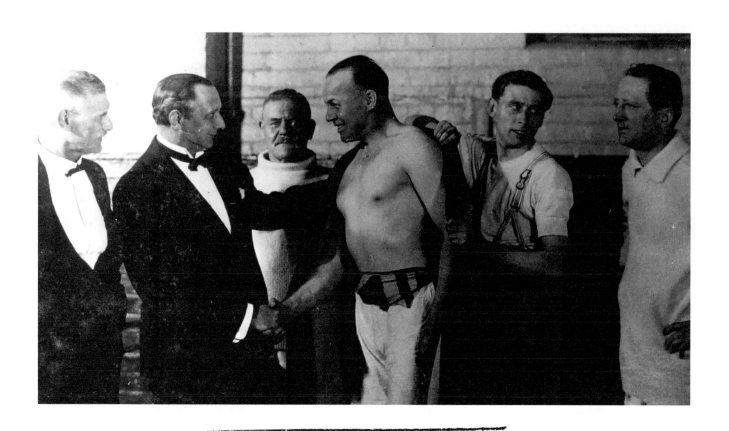

FILM STORIES OF GREAT FIGHTS.

REALISTIC BOXING MATCH.

By THE FILM CRITIC.

The great historical effort of the British Productions, Hove, who are filming famous combats throughout the ages on their actual battle-grounds. and with, as far as possible, the actual armour and weapons used, is nearing its completion, and within the next few weeks the first episode will be ready for the screen

One particular scene that calls for comment is that of the fight which took place at the National Sporting Club between Percy Moran, the producer, and Matt Wells, the ex-light-weight champion boxer of Great Britain. To keep up to the standard of their technical adviser, Mr. Felix Joubert, F.S.A.Scot., who has insisted on the correct methods and ceremony attached to the ancient fights, Mr Percy Moran and Mr Jack Harding have secured a fight picture that will enable them to set an example to American film producers.

Cutting from ___venine Sta___

Dated___2-18___ 192?

Address___Shoe Lane___

FILM NOTES.

PICTORIAL RECORD OF HISTORIC INCIDENT.

BATTLE-AXE COMBAT.

During the last few days a new kind of film has been completed which would convince even Hilaire Belloc that the screen could be utilised for teaching history in an interesting and informative manner. The picture in question is "The Field of Honour," which was shown to the Press and leading authorities last week

The film is the first of a series of pictori cords of historic·incidents, and the one in tion was the battle-axe combat betweer English knight named Thomas Que and a gundian named Jacques Lalaine at Bruge the year, 1445.

Natural Work of Art.

This has been made possible by the faci provided by the Belgian Government, who only placed thousands of Belgian troops at disposal but granted permission for a huge to hold 1000 people to be built in Bruges ma place.

The armour and weapons were supplied Felix Joubert, F.S.A. Scot., the world-fa antiquarian, who is the prime mover in venture, and his unique knowledge of arm matters and the ancient laws of chivalry been used to such an effect that the compl film is a real national asset, retaining as it a pictorial record of a piece of the national tory in which this Empire is unshak founded.

Cutting from

TIMES

Printing House Square, E.C

Date___9'10___ 19

HISTORIC DUELS.

The Field of Honour is the title of an interesting and instructive series of British films which are being prepared by Mr. Felix Joubert, swordsman and authority on ancient weapons and armour, and Mr. Percy Moran, otherwise known in the film world as "Lieutenant Daring." In this series there will be presented some of the famous duels men-

Forger...

There wasn't anything Felix Joubert couldn't make or copy. He was regarded as one of the finest craftsman of his day. His ability to replicate and restore furniture from all periods was handed down to him from Amadée Joubert. With such skills, and a whole array of craftsman at his disposal, the notion of authorship and authenticity becomes hazy. At what point is a copy a fake? Joubert's wording is always careful, but he was certainly a natural storyteller. And sometimes is hard to distinguish between art and artifice.

In 1878, Amadée Joubert and Son made a chimney piece which was exhibited in the Paris Exhibition. In the centre there was an 'alleged original' Holbein. (Paris Exhibition Catalogue, 1878).

The piece was offered for auction in 1925 by Felix Joubert, who was working at Christies at the time. It was sold as an original, only later in 2012 it was reclassified as the 'Circle of Hans Holbein'. It might be worth looking into its real origins...

A forgery in bronze by Felix Joubert representing Geometry and Astrology after a terracotta by the Flemish sculptor, Giovanni Giambologna.

It was acquired by The Victoria and Albert Museum as a known forgery.

Felix Joubert's rare specimen of a 'falchion' "is said to have belonged possibly to Joan of Arc". Joubert made the claim based on a medal which pictures the saint carrying a similar sword...

Top left: Portrait of a Lady 'Circle of Hans Holbein II', Provenance Felix Joubert anonymous sale, 12th June 1925, sold as 'Early Flemish School
Middle left: An Allegory of History, Joubert, Felix, From the Victoria and Albert Museum archive. Museum number A. 67-1953

Bottom left: 'A rare falchion sword of the 15th century, which lends some probability that it may have been the original sword of Joan of Arc.' The Graphic, 12 February, 1926

A rare falchion sword of the early 15th century, discovered in a château near Domremy in Lorraine, which lends some probability to the belief that it may have been the original sword of Joan of Arc. It is worth noting, in this connection, that a medal struck in commemoration of the Maid, in the Bibliothèque National at Paris, represents her carrying a sword identical with this unusual type.

And more...

In the 1920s Felix Joubert was commissioned to make furniture for Queen Mary's Doll House. Edwin Lutyens designed the famous doll's house, which is now owned by Queen Elizabeth II. One of Felix's first tenants, Sir William Nicholson provided murals for the house as did Edmund Dulac. Joubert also produced tiny arms and armour for the house which was completed in 1924.

'If you can draw hands you can draw anything'

Felix Joubert

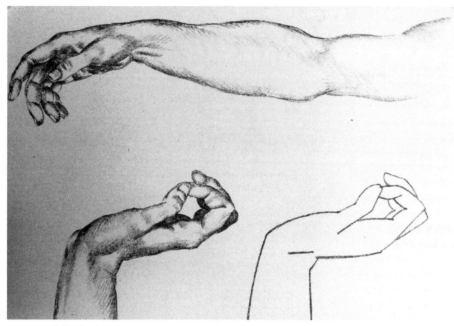

Felix Joubert's study of hands. Courtesy of his grandson, Mike Bell.

Felix was a champion fencer and expert of medieval arms and armour. He restored and forged armour in a foundry he installed at the back of The Pheasantry.

In 1916 fellow fencing expert Lord Howard de Walden commissioned him to design a trench knife, famously known as The Welsh Knife. Never afraid to spin a story, Joubert claimed the knife that was distributed to the 9th Battalion of Royal Welsh Fusiliers was based on 'The well known and historic Welsh Cledd'.

Joubert also made tapestries for de Walden and fitted him in a full suit of armour for the Chelsea Arts Ball.

Sculptor

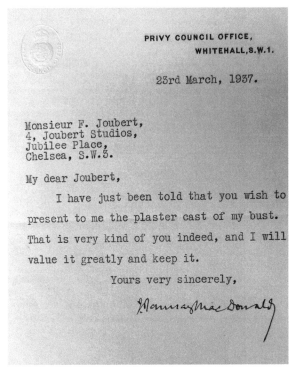

PRIVY COUNCIL OFFICE,
WHITEHALL,S.W.1.

23rd March, 1937.

Monsieur F. Joubert,
4, Joubert Studios,
Jubilee Place,
Chelsea, S.W.3.

My dear Joubert,

    I have just been told that you wish to present to me the plaster cast of my bust. That is very kind of you indeed, and I will value it greatly and keep it.

        Yours very sincerely,

        Ramsay MacDonald

'Felix Joubert, the sculptor, was one of the latest to make a portrait of Ramsey Macdonald before that statesman's death. Joubert divides his time between his home in Chelsea and his beautiful villa in Antibes. He is an accomplished fencer and a fine judge of armour. He has advised Christies on this subject, and he himself got together a fine collection of armour which he presented to the museum at Nice.

The Artist 15 January 1938

A stone fountain 'From the Source'. One of many stone statues to be produced by Joubert Studios.

35

W. Nicholson, 'Carlina', 1909, Many believe this to be a portrait of Nicholson's lover, Marie Laquelle. © Desmond Banks

Lovers of The Pheasantry

Charles Sykes, 'The Spirit of Ecstasy', or
'Miss Thornton in her Nightie'.

J.W.B.

A view of Benjamin Nicholson at the Pheasantries

Nicholson by E.O. Hoppé 1912   Nicholson Lustre Bowl, 1911 © Courtesy Desmond Banks

Sir William Nicholson

By the time Sir William Nicholson arrived at The Pheasantry in 1902, he had established his career as part of 'The Beggerstaffs' with brother-in-law, James Pryde. Together they produced ground -breaking poster designs, and William Nicholson was also individually known for his innovative woodcuts.

But now he would turn his full attention to painting, and so he rented a studio at The Pheasantry from Felix Joubert, who was letting out all of the house as apartments and studios. Nicholson could invite his society patrons to come and sit for him and produced some of his finest work at his Pheasantry studio. As well as portraits, he painted some of his most radiant still lifes, and numerous paintings of his mistress and housekeeper at The Pheasantry, Marie Laquelle (Adèle Marie Scheistel).

The future Prime Minister, Sir Winston Churchill was one of Nicholson's pupils. Sir Winston recalled, 'the person who taught me the most about painting was William Nicholson'.

The noted contemporary artist Ben Nicholson, who was to become one of the leading figures of modern British painting, often visited his father at The Pheasantry, where he is pictured at the easel, working on a canvas under the watchful eye of his father (Pictured opposite in a cartoon by Beggerstaffs).

In 1909 fellow artist Augustus John painted Nicholson's portrait:

'I have started Nicholson - as a set off to his rare beauty I am putting in a huge nude girl at his side. This will add interest I feel'

Augustus John, Letter to Lady Ottoline Morrell, Jan 1909

Augustus John considered it one of his finest portraits. Nicholson was equally pleased with it and for many years it hung on the walls of his Pheasantry studio. There is no 'nude girl' in the finished painting, but one of the artist's landscapes instead.

'John's snapshot of me is capital and I think everyone else seems to agree'

William Nicholson, 1909

'On one of the walls of The Pheasantry hung the fine, belligerent portrait of William by John, who... had said he would like to paint William, but could not afford to do it unless commissioned. William commissioned it for a very small sum, making the stipulation that if anyone bought it he would give the difference in price to John...'

'A was an Artist'

Marguerite Steen, 'William Nicholson'.

Nicholson eventually sold the painting to The Fitzwilliam Museum for a thousand pounds, which he split with John.

In 1896 James McNeil Whistler recommended William Nicholson to a publisher who commissioned a series of woodcuts: *'An Alphabet'. 'A is for Artist'* woodcut by William Nicholson © Desmond Banks.

Opposite page: Augustus John's portrait of William Nicholson. © Augustus John Estate/ Bridgeman Images. Photograph © Fitzwilliam Museum.

Le Bonnet Tricolore, 1910, courtesy Desmond Banks

'A thin, pretty, sharp-faced young Provençale, with a pair of dark- blue eyes full of feminine slyness, and exquisite colouring...'

Marie, 1910, courtesy Desmond Banks

Marie Laquelle

The story goes, Nicholson first saw Adèle Marie Scheistel months before they finally met when she was brought to his studio to model for him. He was bewitched from the start. His future partner Marguerite Steen recounts in her biography of William:

"One morning, from the top of a bus in the King's Road, William noticed on the pavement the neat, fresh, spring-like figure of a young woman, obviously bound on her household shopping. The driver of the bus caught William's eye and pointed with his whip. "There's a pretty thing to see on a May morning".

Nicholson encouraged his new mistress and housekeeper at The Pheasantry to change her name to Marie Laquelle. Marie stayed with Nicholson at The Pheasantry until 1916, when he was evicted for non payment of rent. Nicholson painted Marie many times, and also was to paint her daughter, Georgette, and Georgette's second husband, Norman holder. Nicholson remained friends with Marie after his second marriage, and financially supported her for many years. She died in May 1949, two weeks before Nicholson.

The Spirit of Ecstasy

'I fell in love with her at first sight but as I couldn't marry her I felt I must keep away as much as I could... Before long, we discovered we loved each other intensely and our scruples vanished before our great love'

Lord John Montagu of Beaulieu

Eleanor Thornton

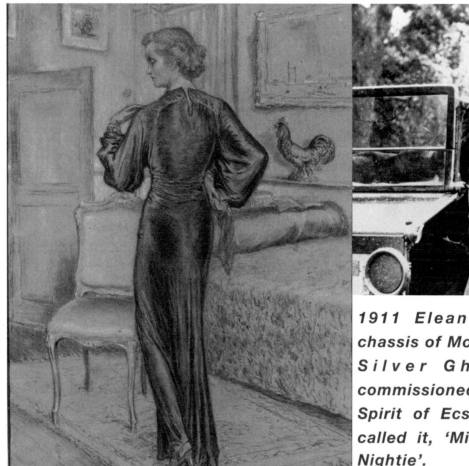

1911 Eleanor poses on the chassis of Montagu's Rolls Royce Silver Ghost, Montagu commissioned the mascot 'The Spirit of Ecstasy' or as friends called it, 'Miss Thornton in her Nightie'.

Eleanor Thornton was born in 1880 in Stockwell. She left school at 16, taking a job at the Automobile Club (now the RAC). It was here she met Tory MP and motoring enthusiast, Lord John Montagu of Beaulieu.

When Lord Montagu launched his glossy magazine, 'The Car Illustrated' in 1902, Eleanor became his private secretary and mistress and began living in The Pheasantry. In a letter to his daughter John Montagu wrote:

'I fell in love with her at first sight but as I couldn't marry her I felt I must keep away as much as I could... Before long, we discovered we loved each other intensely and our scruples vanished before our great love'.

'Eleanor Thornton led a double life. During the day she worked in Lord Montagu's office and in the evening she returned to The Pheasantry, which, under the ownership of the Jouberts, had become the centre of a vibrant artists' colony, 'Thorny'. as she was known to her friends, became a favourite model of the artist Charles Sykes. He was commissioned by Lord Montagu to design a personal mascot for his Rolls Royce and used Eleanor as his model for the iconic "Spirit of Ecstasy".' (Lord Montagu's biographer, P. Tritton).

In 1903 Eleanor gave birth to Montagu's daughter, Joan. The child was put up for adoption to avoid scandal.

There have been many accounts of their love, but no words have survived in Eleanor's own hand other than correspondence with Montage's wife, Lady Cecil. The women discuss the upcoming voyage where Eleanor was to accompany Montagu to India in 1915.

In a letter to Lady Cecil, Eleanor writes:

"You have the satisfaction to know that he will be well looked after. I do not think for one moment there will be trouble in the Med, but supposing?... The Lord will have an extra chance, for there will be my place in the boat for him, even if he has to be stunned to take it."

Montagu and Eleanor boarded the S.S. Persia in Marseilles on Christmas Day, 1915. Five days into the voyage they were having lunch when the ship was torpedoed by a German U- boat. Montagu survived, as arrangements had been made for him to have a life vest sewn into his suit. Eleanor's body was never found.

Before his death Montagu arranged to have a letter delivered to his daughter, Joan.

My darling Joan,

If you ever have to open this letter it will probably be because I am no longer in this world... So I tell you who I am; who you know as 'Uncle' now, and why I love you so much, both for your own sake, and for your mother's sake. I am your father, whom you met at Windsor last summer...

About 1900 I first met your mother, three years before you were born. I fell in love with her at first sight but as I couldn't marry her I kept away from her as much as I could...

Finally in 1902, in February, she became my secretary, and together we started The Car and put our whole energies into the new venture. Before one we discovered that we loved each other intensely and our mutual scruples vanished before our great love...

Your mother was the most wonderful and lovable woman I have ever met. She showed me for 14 years a devotion which is beyond description and loved as few women love, I equally loved her as few men love.

Goodbye darling Joan. God bless you always.

Your loving father,

Montagu of Beaulieu.

Edith Holden

Edith Holden and her husband Alfred Earnest Smith, (also an artist and sculptor) lived at The Pheasantry following their wedding in 1911. The couple moved into the Pheasantry to escape the disdain of her family, who disapproved of her marrying a man seven years her junior.

She drowned in the Thames near Kew on the evening of 16th March 1920, as she reached for a branch of chestnut blossom, or at least that is how the newspapers reported it.

Edith had never intended her 1906 journal to be published; she had written them to inspire a love of nature in her students. But in 1976 her great-niece, who had grown up looking at Edith's diary, showed it to a publisher at a party. The following year it was published and it has since become a cult classic.

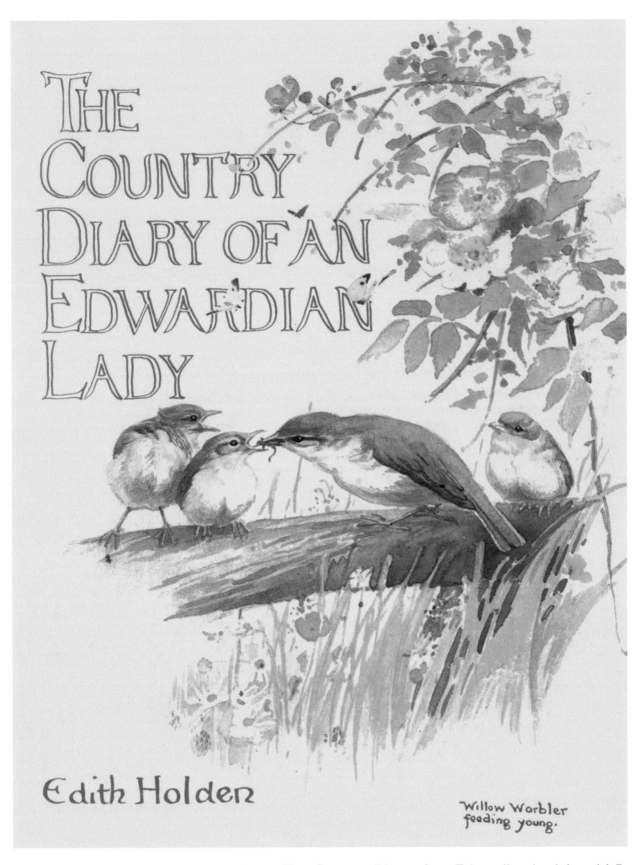

THE
COUNTRY
DIARY OF AN
EDWARDIAN
LADY

Edith Holden

Willow Warbler
feeding young.

When it was first published in 1977, 'The Country Diary of an Edwardian Lady', sold 5 million copies in 13 languages. It has been reprinted countless times since.

MADAME SERAPHINE ASTAFIEVA

The world-renowned Russian dancer, as the Queen of Sheba, the character in which she will be seen in the pageant at the Yp

A Princess and her Dancers

In 1916 Princess Seraphina Astafieva opened her Russian Dancing Academy at The Pheasantry. Grand niece of Count Tolstoy, and daughter of Prince Alexander Astafiev, she trained at the Bolshoi and Marinsky ballet schools, and later joined the Russian impresario, Sergei Diaghilev's, *Ballet Russes,* escaping an unhappy second marriage.

The outbreak of the First World War stranded her in London, where she was playing Cleopatra, a role she first danced in Paris opposite Nijinsky. Unable to tour, she started her own ballet school at The Pheasantry. Astafieva was known as a great mime - an acting dancer. Emphasis on emotional truth was at the core of her teaching, alongside technique. Her name has been left out of many accounts and biographies. This was noted by one of her most famous pupils, Sir Anton Dolin,

'What a wonderful woman she was! There is not an English dancer of repute who has not studied with her and paid, or not paid, for what they learnt. And yet how little we read in books about Astafieva'.

Sir Anton Dolin, *'Autobiography'.*

It is strange she should be forgotten as she was responsible for the success of many accomplished dancers and was a key figure in the birth of British ballet.]

'She had settled in London in 1914, the first great Russian artiste to open a studio in England, where she proved that British dancers could make a mark for themselves if they had the right training'.

Sir Anton Dolin, *'Markova, Her Life and Art'*

THE CREATOR OF "CLÉOPÂTRE"
Now Teaching Dancing in London.

Bertram Park

MLLE. SERAPHINE ASTAFIEVA

The famous Russian dancer, who in her own land is as well known as Pavlova, and who was for some time the bright particular star of the Russian Ballet in both Petrograd and Moscow. She has now established a school of dancing in London which is securing a great success. Mlle. Astafieva has established an international reputation, as prior to the war she was known in almost

"OUR DAY" AND OUR ALLY

A Famous and Beautiful Russian Dancer who will Appear at the Empire Matinée.

E. O. Hoppe

MADAME SERAFINE ASTAFIEVA

Above: Léon Bakst's design for 'Cleopatre', played by Astafieva in 1914 for The Ballet Russes. Opposite page- cartoon by Helen McKie showing Serafina Astafieva from 'The Bystander' June 1917 'A Swinburne Ballet' produced at The Lyric Theatre for the 'Concerts at the Front Fund, WW1'. Insert Astafieva performing her knife dance in the same ballet.

A Swinburne Ballet

THE BACCHANALE

ALEX GOUDIN

MME ASTAFIEVA IN THE SWORD DANCE.

ALEX GOUDIN & MLLE MIKOULINA

HELEN

[N

A GREAT RUSSIAN DANC
Which Originated at a Charity Matiné

MLLE. S

Mlle. Seraphine Astafieva, who is one of Russia's most famous dancers, has been appearing as première danseuse in the Swinburne
established an international reputation, as prior to the war she was known in almost every European capital. In private life she is
Court. One of Mlle Astafieva's greatest triumphs in Londo

Ph

IN THE SWINBURNE BALLET

d Enjoyed Huge Success at the Coliseum.

E ASTAFIEVA

ch was first produced at a charity matinée at the Lyric Theatre and later included in the bill at the Coliseum. Mlle. Astafieva
M. Greaves, who is a high official connected with the Russian Red Cross, and who was also one of the chamberlains at the late Imper
reation of the title-rôle in the ballet, "Cléopâtre." at Covent Garden

ertram Park

Serafina Astafieva's poets

In 1916 Ezra Pound introduced TS Eliot to Serafina Astafieva, with the specific intention that he might use her as 'a muse' to inspire a poem. *'Whispers of Immortality'* was the result. Pound was disappointed by his depiction of Astafieva as 'Grishkin', and alludes to Eliot's portrait in his *'Pisan Cantos':*

'Grishkin's photo refound years after

With the feeling that Mr. Eliot may have

missed something, after all, in composing his vignette'.

Ezra Pound, Canto 78, 73-75

Perhaps Pound believed Eliot would have more to say about Astafieva's importance as an interpreter and celebrant of ancient dance traditions. Pound celebrates her work as a dancer, and as an upholder of an ancient tradition of dance:

'A little flame for a little

Conserved in the Imperial ballet, never danced in a theatre

'Or Astafieva inside the street doors of the Wigmore'

'So Astafieva had conserved the tradition

From Byzance and before then'.

Ezra Pound, Pisan Cantos 77, line 466-467 and Canto 79, lines 484, 489

According to Ezra Pound's biographer, Humphrey Carpenter, Pound recalled a dance of Astafieva called 'Spermatopyros' about the making of the seed of life, the 'female equivalent of sperm' which turns into fire. There is so much meaning hidden in Pound's lines but his relationship with Astafieva is not documented further.

Whispers of Immortality

Grishkin is nice: her Russian eye

Is underlined for emphasis;

Uncorseted, her friendly bust

Gives promise of pneumatic bliss.

The couched Brazilian jaguar

Compels the scampering marmoset

With subtle effluence of cat;

Grishkin has a maisonette;

The sleek Brazilian jaguar

Does not in its arboreal gloom

Distil so rank a feline smell

As Grishkin in a drawing-room.

And even the Abstract Entities

Circumambulate her charm;

But our lot crawls between dry ribs

To keep our metaphysics warm.

T.S. Eliot Whispers of Immortality (1915-1918)

'One morning, Astafieva told us that she was expecting Diaghileff to come to the studio... we were all keyed up with excitement at the prospect of a possible engagement... Diaghileff entered the studio. He was met by Seraphine, whom he kissed affectionately'.

Sir Anton Dolin, Autobiography.

Savoy Hotel
London. W. C. 2.

July 9th 1925

Madame Seraphine Astafieva,
152, King s Rd,
Chelsea. S. W. 3.

Chere amie,

I am **very** glad at the thought that my acceptance of
the patronage of your school might be helpful to you and useful.

The display bill that you have shown **me** is **very** well
arranged and suitable for the purpose.

There is one thing I should like to point out to you at
at your school.
this early moment, and that is that I must ask you to bar all
elements who have broken engagements made with my enterprises, or
where re-engagements were not entered into on account of differ-
ences with the Management of the Russian Ballet.

Yours sincerely,

Astafieva in her Pheasantry Studio with pupils. Photographer unknown.

Alongside teaching, Serafina Astafieva continued to perform and choreograph for various productions including Diaghilev and Thomas Beecham in 'Le Coq d'Or'. She also appeared in many charity performances such as The Swinburne Ballet in 1916 and the Ypres Ball and Eastern Revel in 1922.

Cover of Handbill for Ypres Ball 30 November 1922, Courtesy Royal Albert Hall Archive

DRAWN BY F. MATANIA

THE QUEEN OF SHEBA IN "THE EASTERN QUEENS" PAGEANT AT THE YPRES BALL

This ball, held last week at the Albert Hall, was an undoubted success, many prominent members of London society participating in the dancing and in the "Eastern Revels." The feature of the evening was the procession of "Eastern Queens of the Ancient World," and above our artist has drawn the scene after the arrival of the Queen of Sheba (Princess Astafieva) and her attendants (pupils of the Russian School of Dancing) from the great pillared doorway at the back of the hall to her throne in the centre. Amongst the dancers during the evening some fine costumes were seen, those of Lord and Lady Ossulston, as a Courtier and Lady of the Eighteenth Century, being especially attractive

a

Review with illustration by Matania 1922, and programme, Courtesy Royal Albert Hall Archive.

PROGRAMME—continued

10

SHEBA

March Indienne - - *Sellenick*

by the Massed Bands

Makeda (Queen of Sheba)	Princess Astafieva
Miss Lolita Hamilton	Miss Claire Divina
Miss Joan Morgan	Miss Marjorie Daw
Miss Carter	Miss Murielle Marise
Miss Connie Taylor	Miss Queenie Neat
Miss Sylvia Willoughby	Miss Betty Prager
Mrs. Booth	Master Fleurent

Africans - M. Fleurent and M. Pease.

Attendants - Pupils of the Russian School of Dancing.

The Ypres Ball

Rehearsals for The Ypres Ball, 1922, showing Alicia Markova (centre middle), in the studio at The Pheasantry

Ypres Ball 30 November 1922, with Astafieva as The Queen of Sheba, surrounded by her pupils. Courtesy Royal Albert Hall Archive

Astafieva with her pupils inside her Pheasantry studio.

Serafina Astafieva's Pupils

Anton Dolin, 1924 photograph unknown

Sir Anton Dolin

One of Astafieva's most devoted pupils, Dolin went on to write many tributes to his teacher. Dolin first saw Astafieva dance in the Swinburne Ballet in 1916, and was determined to study with her. He was one of Astafieva's resident pupils and recalled:

'Night after night I would sit up late listening to Astafieva and to the stories she would tell of her life in Russia, the school and the dancers'.

Anton Dolin's partnership with Alicia Markova began in The Pheasantry Studio. It has been described as one of the greatest ballet partnerships of all time. In 1935, they formed the Markova-Dolin Ballet company, and in 1950 the London Festival Ballet which was later renamed The English National Ballet.

Markova by Gordon Anthony, 1935

Photograph c. 1936 © Constantine.

Dame Alicia Markova

London born Lily Alicia Marks started training at The Pheasantry at the age of ten. The story of her mother's initial meeting with Astafieva has been recounted many times, including this recollection by future founder of The Royal Ballet School, Arnold Haskell:

'One day my mother returned from the class in great excitement. There had been quite a scene- "Was it more than the usual scandal? Was it by any chance a Bolshoi scandal?" "Yes, it could be called that."

It appears that a very beautiful young woman had brought a timid and skinny girl for an audition. While the child was getting undressed, the mother had handed Astafieva a card- and then came the explosion. Mother and child were turned out and told in a mixture of Russian and English never to darken the Pheasantry doors again. The words printed on that card were, Alicia, the miniature Pavlova'...

Fortunately for ballet, for Alicia and for me the mother plucked up sufficient courage to return with her child, more than ever convinced that Astafieva was the one teacher who could develop Alicia. She relented, saw the child dance, was greatly impressed and accepted her on the spot.'

Arnold Haskell, Balletomania

"As a teacher Astafieva had an inventive brain and devised most remarkable combinations of steps for her pupils. She prepared such difficult material for us and steered us through it so skilfully that no other choreographer scared us when we went out into the world to make our way as ballet dancers. We knew instinctively that we would be able to master his ballet, no matter how complicated it might be. I have always managed to adapt myself to the demands made by all the different choreographers I have encountered, and I thank my early Astafieva training for it".

Dame Alicia Markova

The Young Markova, photographer unknown.

"*Your little girl is like a racehorse; you must take great care of her and keep her wrapped up in cotton wool.*"

Astafieva invited the impresario Diaghilev to watch her dance and she was offered a place with his Ballet Russes at the age of 14. She changed her name to Alicia Markova, just as fellow pupil Patrick Kay was to become Anton Dolin. "Who would pay to see Alicia Marks?" Sergei Diaghilev had asked her. Alicia Markova was to become one of the most important and popular figures in English Ballet.

She was the first English ballerina to become a principal dancer of a ballet company, and with another of Astafieva's pupils, Dame Margot Fonteyn, is one of only two British dancers to be recognised as Prima Ballerina Assoluta.

Tremendously famous during her life time, she appeared with Bob Hope and Buddy Holly and the Crickets, and had her own radio programme and was even asked to judge the Miss World contest in Paris. Her dancing partnership with fellow pupil Anton Dolin spanned many years and helped spread the appeal of ballet internationally.

Arnold Haskell

My education for my life's work had begun with Alicia's first grip on the Pheasantry barre'.

Arnold Haskell "Balletomane".

Arnold Haskell was a self confessed 'balletomane' (a word he introduced into the English language for ballet aficionados). He would visit The Pheasantry to watch Astafieva's pupils, including Alicia Markova. When in 1924 Alicia's father died suddenly, Arnold's mother sponsored her lessons. Arnold went on to marry Alicia's younger sister, Vivienne.

'I found my way to the studio form time to time and was always fascinated by the highly organised chaos of her method of teaching as well as by the wise remarks given in her picturesque jargon. She had male pupils, which was almost unknown at that time, among them Rupert Doone and a very brilliant Irish boy, Patrick Kay, some years before his incarnation as Anton Dolin'.

Arnold Haskell

Haskell became a ballet critic, co-founder of the Camargo Society, director and headmaster of The Royal Ballet School. And has been celebrated for his work to establish a national ballet in the UK.

A bronze bust of Astafieva by Emmy Haskell.

Phyllis Bedells

Phyllis Bedells was the first British Prima Ballerina at The London Empire. She was a founding member of The Royal Academy of Dance in 1920 and appeared as a soloist with the Vic- Wells Ballet.

Joan Lawson

Joan Lawson went on to become a well known dancer, teacher and dance writer. She danced with the Nemchina- Dolin company and went on to teach at the Royal Ballet School.

Annette Mills

Sister of renowned actor John Mills, Edith Mabel Mills began training as a pianist before studying dance in Astafieva's studio. Her dancing career was cut short by injury. She then began composing and had numerous hits during the Second World War, including 'Boomps a daisy' and 'Home Sweet Home', but is best remembered for her appearance in the BBC television series 'Muffin the Mule', between 1946 and 1955, in which she appeared and wrote the music.

Anna Neagle

Voted Britains most popular film star in 1949, Anna Neagle performed countless musical and period roles on stage and screen, including her renowned performance of Nell Gwynn in 1934, and Queen Victoria in Queen Victoria the Great in 1937.

Photographs on these pages- all by Bassano Ltd © National Portrait Gallery.

E.O.Hoppé, Hermione Darnborough, 1933 © Curatorial Assistance, Inc/ E.O Hoppé Estate Collection

Hermione Darnborough

In 1929 Astafieva arranged for Darnborough to audition for Sergei Diaghilev at her studio in The Pheasantry. He was impressed with the 14 year old's ability and asked to see her in three years time. He died before this came about, so Astafieva encouraged her to join Fonteyn at Sadler's Wells in 1934. In the same year, while still in her teens, she posed nude for German born photographer E.O. Hoppé.

One of the foremost teachers of dancing today is Mme. Astafieva, who created the roles of Cleopatra and Scheherazade at Covent Garden when they were presented by M. Diaghileff in 1914. In 1915 she settled in London and established a school here (after seeing what remarkable dancers the English were). She now has pupils with M. Diaghileff at the Alhambra, with Anna Pavlova, the Swedish Ballet, and other companies. Miming is taught and performed with perfect time and precision.

THE LONDON ILLUSTRATED NEWS Dec 31 1921
Drawings by Steven Spurrier

Dame Margot Fonteyn

'It was to Astafieva's studio in the Pheasantry, Chelsea that Mrs
Hookham took Fonteyn... because she had been the teacher of
Markova and Dolin. Astafieva, already ill and tired of teaching, was
unwilling to accept new pupils, and it was only after Mrs Hookham
had begged her to do so, pleading that her daughter had come all
the way from China to study with her, that Madame agreed that
Fonteyn should come to her classes. Soon she came to think highly
of her new pupil, gave her private lessons as well, and took a great
deal of trouble over her. Fonteyn so loved those lessons that it was
with difficulty that she was persuaded by her mother to consider
going to Sadler's Wells. Astafieva gave her much, but not enough:
not enough strength, not enough discipline; and above all, there was
no direct road from her studio to the stage. So an audition was asked
for... and a day or two later Mrs Hookham has a letter to say her
daughter had been accepted as a student of the Sadler's wells ballet
school'.*

Evelyn Leith, (1945) Ballerina

In 1931 Mrs Hookham secured dancing lessons with Serafina
Astafieva for her daughter, Peggy. Despite being very ill with cancer,
Astafieva taught Peggy in her studio for six months, where her new
pupil received extra tuition from Alicia Markova, who was much
admired by the young dancer. Soon Peggy would change her name
to Margot Fonteyn. She was to succeed Alicia Markova as Prima
Ballerina in the Vic- Wells ballet in 1935, the company that went on
to become The Royal Ballet. Like Markova before her she was
appointed Prima Ballerina absolute by Queen Elizabeth II.

Margot Fonteyn, Bassano 1935 ©National Portrait Gallery

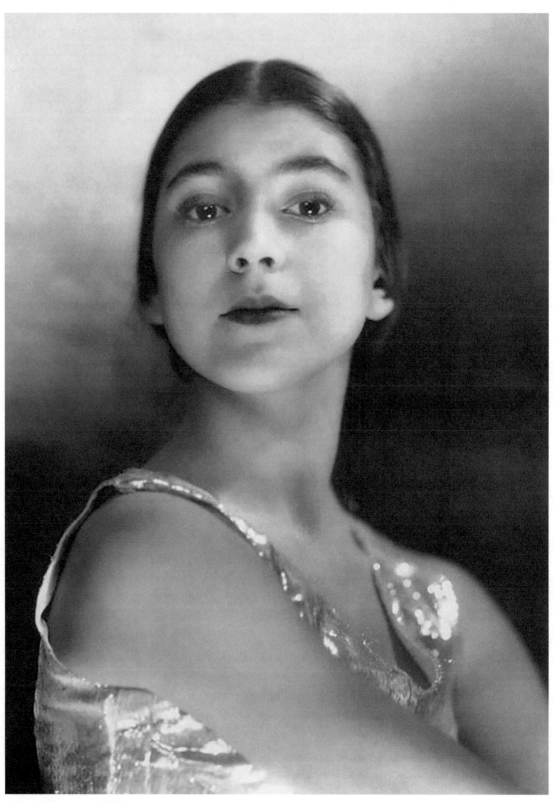

Margot Fonteyn, 1935.
© 2011 Curatorial Assistance, Inc. / E.O. Hoppé Estate Collection

Margot Fonteyn 1955, sketch by Pietro Annigoni.

BRITISH GIRLS *CAN* DANCE

By PRINCESSE SERAPHINE ASTAFIEVA

Principal of the Chelsea Academy of Russian Dancing, whose team of twelve British girls won the International Cup at the first dancing Olympiad in Paris recently.

Where did this fallacy originate- that British girls cannot dance?

Obsessed with the idea that to be a dancer one must be Russian, the British public ignore the wonderful talents of their own girl artists. They do not realise that two essentials, and two alone, go to the making of a dancer- a well proportioned body and correct training methods. Given these, with a genuine love of every art, girls of every nationality have equal opportunities of winning fame on stage or dancing floor.

And what tremendous natural advantages your British girls possess. Beautifully proportioned, they seem built to become a nation of dancers. "But" croaks the pessimist, "British girls have not the true artistic temperament."

How such remarks infuriate me. For what is this "temperament" but the instinct to express thoughts, ideas and emotions in movement? To argue that from childhood the English girl is trained to suppress her feelings is beside the point. Ate the outset this inbred reserve fetters the artist but it cannot stifle creative instinct. For in every one of us smoulders the latent power of self- expression. It is for the teacher, searching her pupils inner consciousness, to coax the spark into a blaze.

Technical ability one will never raise a dancer above the level of an efficient machine. True poetry of movement combines perfect technique with sincere and sympathetic interpretation of the human emotions.

And here in my mind lies the secret of the British dancer's failure. At the expense of intensive technical study, the emotional side of her training is too often neglected, permitting her innate reserve to interpose between the artist and her chance of success.

And undoubtedly the British public is prejudiced against native dancers. Many fine artists have been compelled to adopt foreign names in order to gain an audience. Sokolova, Butsova, Anton Dolin- are all famous, all are British. Is it not strange that while plain Mary Johnson might dance divinely for years unnoticed, yet as Marya Ivanova she would draw a full house?

But, step by step, British artists are dancing their way to recognition. Only last month English girls carried off the International Cup against all comers at the Paris Dancing Olympiad. British competitors secured every title- amateur, professional, and mixed - in the recent world's ballroom championships. And both Charleston and acrobatic dancing honours are held by British couples.

It is true that England has not as yet produced a world- famous ballerina. But without money and influential backing, even genius could not launch a Pavlova.

Barriers of prejudice are destroyed, however, I foresee a wonderful future for British dancers. Sooner or later, the public must realise and acclaim their supremacy. And when that time comes, I feel confident that a British Pavlova will be found- an artist worthy yo uphold the reputation of British dancing before the whole world.

С. А. АСТАФЬЕВА   S. ASTAPHIEVE

1916 caricature of Serafina Astafieva, Nicolas and Sergei Legat

KING'S ROAD—continued.

52 THE PHEASANTRY :
Pheasantry Club (Reny De Meo, manager). See advertisement
1 Russian Academy of Dancing (Madame Seraphine Astafieva)
2 Watkin & Beach Misses, artists
3 Madeley Miss R.M.S. artist
4 Gill R. R
6 Bater Kenneth
9 McKie Miss Helen
0 Bell Ivor Campbell

162 Howells David & Son, clothiers & outfitters; fancy dress costumes for hire. Tel. Flaxman 7736. See advert

........*here is Jubilee pl*.........

164 RADNOR MANSION :

1 Conway-Poole Maj. Wm. Thos
2 Digby Miss
3 Quartier H

———

164 Lloyds Bank Ltd. (W.

178 Bull Arth. & Co. ho
178A, Miriam (Gown Robes) Ltd

BLENHEIM HOUSE :
1 Lepere Miss
3 Jones W. R. D.S.O
4 Haig Mrs
5 Crossley Maj. B. C
6 Lovell E. G
7 Jones Miss
8 Scaramanga Jn
9 Wood Mrs. Edmnd
10 Fortlage Mrs
11 D'Arcy Mrs

The Pheasantry Club

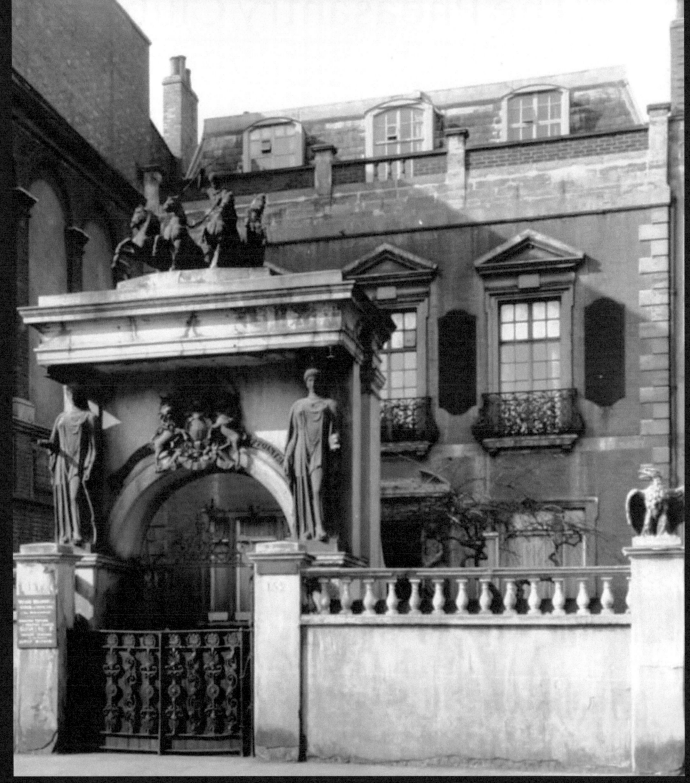

The Pheasantry in 1937, photographer unknown.

E.O.Hoppé

At The Bar in the Pheasantry Club,

"Bohemia" series, London 1935

'In the heart of Chelsea, famous haunt for artists and writers is the Pheasantry Club. The premises are in the building that was originally the hunting lodge of Charles II- the story goes that it was one of his trysting places with Nell Gwynn.

Every inch of wall space in the Pheasantry is devoted to art. Paintings etchings, pastels, gouaches, charcoal drawings- every medium is on display, and any empty spots are bulging with statuary'.

Holiday Magazine.

In 1932 Felix Joubert officially retired, handing over the running of the studios and basement to René De Meo and his wife, artist and actress, Pamela Synge. In the basement the couple founded a private members club.

Felix and Blanche were its first members as their grandson, Mike Bell explains, "they had an underground passageway joining their library in Turret House with the club. So Joubert had no choice but to make them its first members."

Italo Renato Ulisse De Meo, was a charismatic Italian who had tried many trades before he started running The Pheasantry Club. His Pheasantry Club attracted an extraordinary array of artists, writers, actors, and politicians including Humphrey Bogart and Lauren Bacall, Augustus John, Dylan and Caitlin Thomas, Francis Bacon and Lucian Freud to name but a few of its regulars.

De Meo acquired a huge collection of artworks which hung on the walls of the club from patrons including Augustus John, Pietro Annigoni, and even the infamous Marchesa Casati, there were gilded mirrors and carvings by Joubert, and murals by Pheasantry resident, Helen Mckie. Artist and future Pheasantry resident and club member, Timothy Whidborne, recalled how De Meo, and later his partner and successor, Mario Cazzani, often accepted artworks as payment for bills.

Numerous sketches and paintings by Augustus John and Pietro Annigoni have since been sold at auction, provenance: Pheasantry Club.

THE 1930's

De Meo after his portrait by Annigoni

'The life and Soul of the Club is De Meo, whom the English love to call 'René'. It is he that we find there, in the evening, triumphing on the stage of his bar, sometimes camouflaged in improvised clothing, addressing his usual clients in all languages, without remotely offending, but rather soliciting from them the maddest of laughter'.

1939 'Guida Degli Italiani In Gran Bretagna'.

René De Meo

'René on those evenings would welcome them with his own Italian cooking and wide smile like a brilliant Italian sky.

There, Aneurin argued with Italian socialists one week, and Italian tenors the next and acquired his long and lasting interest in the whole Italian scene'.

Michael Foot, 'Aneurin Bevan: A Biography'.

'René was a great lover of opera, and The Pheasantry was a haunt of Italian opera singers.'

John Joel, 'I paid the Piper'.

According to the musical agent, John Joel, René represented the Italian opera star Luigi Infantino. Nesta McDonald also remembers another Italian opera singer, Beniamino Gigli singing in the Club.

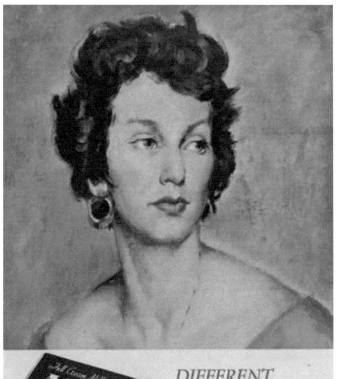

DIFFERENT...

for her, AERO–the milk chocolate that's different!

For a new experience in delightful full-cream milk chocolate that melts in your mouth in a moment.

BY ROWNTREES

Pamela Synge, artist, actress and anonymous model for the Aero Girl poster campaign, 1955. The advert appeared on posters and on television making her face, if not her name, widely recognised. Neslé. James Grant painted Pamela twice and encouraged her to become a painter in her own right.

Pamela Synge

During the early 1950's, Rowntree launched a major advertising campaign for Aero, to relaunch the chocolate bar after the war. Pamela Synge was one of 40 anonymous 'Aero Girls' whose identity was recently revealed by Kerstin Doble and Francesca Taylor.

James Grant painted Pamela De Meo twice in 1955 for Rowntree. Pheasantry club regular, Anthony Devas, (Pamela's cousin), was also asked to paint for the Campaign and Pietro Annigoni drew Pamela.

Pamela trained as a dancer and worked as a model before the war. She attended RADA, and worked for the Red Cross. Her first marriage was very brief, and didn't survive the separation of war, but she had a son, Roland. Later she studied painting at Central Saint Martins and Chelsea College of Arts. She married René de Meo when still only 19, and they had two sons, Philip and Justin.

Her portrait of Rudolph Nureyev was shown at the RA summer show in 1980 and she had work accepted by the Royal Society of Artists and the Paris Salon. After divorcing De Meo she travelled widely and in 1970 married Brain Synge. She died in 2013 in Chelsea.

Augustus John

Painter, Augustus John's early patronage of The Pheasantry attracted many of his circle including artists, sculptors, and poets.

Dylan and Caitlin Thomas

Caitlin Thomas was a teenager when she began modelling for her father's friend, Augustus John. It is said John saw it as his right to sleep with his models. During one of the sittings with Caitlin he took advantage of his position of power:

'Caitlin was brutally initiated by her father's friend, Augustus John, who considered sleeping with teenagers one of the perk of artistic genius'.

Kathryn Hughes, The Daily Telegraph.

It was John who introduced Caitlin to the poet, Dylan Thomas in the spring of 1936. That same night they checked into a hotel in Chelsea where they stayed for several nights, charging their bill to Augustus John's account. Dylan Thomas recalls their *"funny times full of drinks and Augustus and castles and quarrels"* in a letter to Caitlin in August 1936. The couple were married a year later in 1937.

Etching after one of Augustus John's portraits of Caitlin Thomas.

Etching after one of Augustus John's portraits of Dylan Thomas. c.1937

'Flush with one of Dylan's cheques, Caitlin bought an evening dress in Hammersmith Broadway for £5. It was a gaudy music- hall dress with a cheap lace fichu and a body of bright pink shiny taffeta. Caitlin added red ribbons to the neck and in this overdressed dress she looked superb, and reminded Anthony (Devas) of a Valázquez Princess.

Wearing the dress Caitlin made her entrance to the Pheasantry Club. It was our evening resort in the King's Road…The premises below ground gave a false illusion of safety; if it had been hit by a bomb, in all probability everyone would have been buried under masonry. Yet with merry making, the chatter, food, music and dancing, danger could be ignored.

Caitlin danced wildly and sensuously, the pink skirt swirled, her arms swung above the lace fichu; it was a free floor show, an Extra, Extra to everyone's life. Augustus in a corner watched above a pint of beer, and shouted 'Olé. Triumphant in her beauty Caitlin sharpened her wit on Humphrey Brooke. Her most cruel sallies ricochet against his head with a good natured invitation to have another drink. Caitlin and I tried to teach Humphrey to dance. He was so clumsy we made him take his shoes off, and wore them ourselves to protect our feet'.

Nicolette Devas, 'Two Flamboyant Fathers'

In 1942, Anthony Devas painted Caitlin at Markham Square in the pink dress Nicolette describes.

THE 1940's

A young woman enjoys the attention of a soldier in the Pheasantry Club.

Turnbridge/ Stringer

Inside The Pheasantry Club'

London, 1940

The Marchesa Casati, Augustus John. © Alamy

Marchesa Luisa Casati

A frequent visitor to The Pheasantry Club at this time was Luisa, Marchesa Casati di Soncino, a former lover and patron of Augustus John. In her heyday she had commissioned him, and many other artists to paint her portrait, including, Giovanni Boldini, Paolo Troubetzkoy, Adolph de Meyer, Man Ray, Romaine Brooks and Kees van Dongen. She considered herself a living work of art, determined to be immortalised.

Once one of the richest women in Venice, her life was pure performance. In her heyday she walked along the Grand Canal with her pair of pet cheetahs, wore poisonous snakes as jewellery, and had her nude servants painted in gold leaf, frittering away her considerable wealth on spectacular parties in her palace.

The Marchesa Casati, by Romaine Brooks 1920. Private collection. Image in public domain.

Marchesa Casati
Is a living doll
Pinned on my Frisco
Skid row wall

Her eyes are vast
Her skin is shiny
Blue veins
And wild red hair
Shoulders sweet & tiny

Love her
Love her
Sings the sea
Bluely
Moaning
In the Augustus
John
de John
background

Jack Kerouac, *'The 74th Chorus'*.

The once revered society hostess was portrayed by Vivienne Leigh in 'La Contessa', and Ingrid Bergman in 'A Matter of Time'. She appears in the writing of her lover, Gabriele D'Annunzio, who called her 'The Queen of Hell'. She inspired writers Ezra Pound and Tennessee Williams and Beat poet, Jack Kerouac, describes the 1919 Augustus John portrait of her in his 1954 poem, 'San Fransisco Blues'.

'She made her entrance into that room looking wonderful and saying very little. She wasn't beautiful - she was spectacular'.

Quentin Crisp

Casati employed famous designers to make ever more elaborate costumes; In 1910, she appointed Ballet Russes costumier Léon Bakst to design her a new wardrobe, which included outfits for her to appear as a gilded sun goddess, Queen of the Night, Persian princesses and a harlequin.

In 1922 celebrated haute couture designer, Charles Worth, designed the costume 'Light', complete with diamond netting. It took three months to make and cost 20,000 francs.

Her artistic legacy continues as designers continue to find inspiration from her innovative style. John Galliano, Karl Lagerfield, Tom Ford, Alexander McQueen, Alberta Ferretti and Dries Van Noten have all based collections on the Marchesa Casati.

Casati 1922, in a costume by L. Charles Worth. Photographer unknown.

'Casati was known for her propensity to perform exotic dances, including a rendition of a Persian ballet at her Roman villa, where she danced against a backdrop painted by Bakst, flanked by two naked gold-painted men, who stood motionless like statues for the duration of the performance'.

Anna Sutton, 'Infinite Variety'.

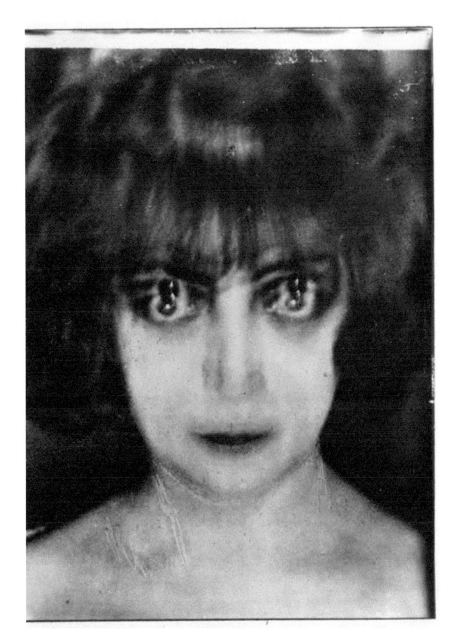

The 1922 image of Marquise Casati helped launch Man Ray's career as a portraitist. It's one of several portraits of Casati by Man Ray. He described her as "acting as if I were doing a movie of her."

"I want to be a living work of art"

Casati was unable to return to Italy or France due to debts she had running into the hundreds of millions. She was living in Chelsea on an allowance offered by Augustus John. Several of her framed collages hung on the walls of the Pheasantry Club.

Collage as seen on the walls of The Pheasantry Club by Luisa Casati

'In one collage, an elegant, old fashioned razor and two ripe peaches with suggestive lobes are juxtaposed with a Gulliverian bejewelled Henry VIII, who dwarfs an entourage of Lilliputian females, all but one with her head snipped off. Other pages featured images of Rasputin and the Duchess of Windsor...'

Judith Thurman, New Yorker

In younger days when Casati's friends suggested she exhibit her journals, but she refused. She was convinced to give them to the owner of the Pheasantry club, René De Meo, for his art collection displayed on the walls of the club. Perhaps as payment of her bill.

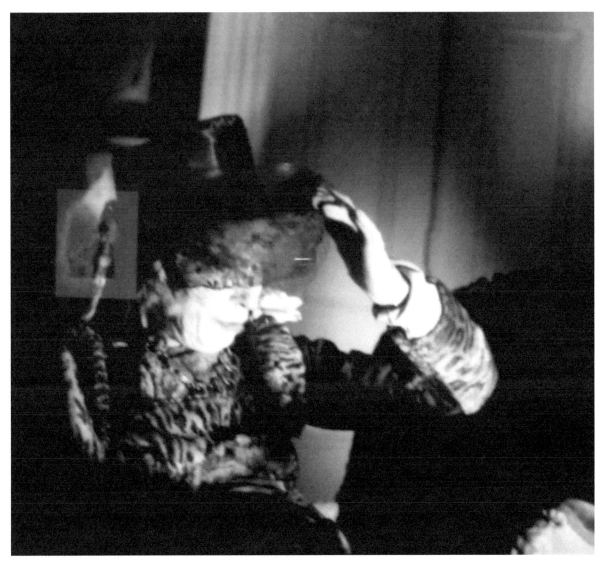
Luisa Casati by Cecil Beaton

'It took all the dignity of the English not to just gawk at this Phantom', says author, Maurice Druon in his 1954 novel, La Volupté d'Être, which was inspired by Casati.

By the late 1950's Casati was living in a one bedroom flat near The Pheasantry, with few remaining friends.

Society photographer, Cecil Beaton visited her in Chelsea and took these pictures. The woman who once demanded the worlds attention, now hides her face from the camera.

Soon after these were taken she died of a stroke and was buried in The Brompton Cemetery.

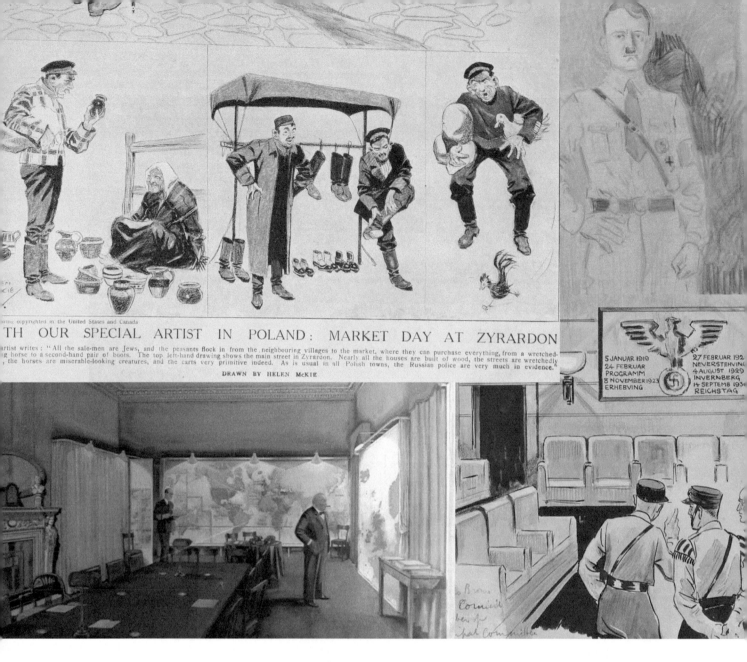

WITH OUR SPECIAL ARTIST IN POLAND: MARKET DAY AT ZYRARDON

Our artist writes: "All the sale-men are Jews, and the peasants flock in from the neighbouring villages to the market, where they can purchase everything, from a wretched-looking horse to a second-hand pair of boots. The top left-hand drawing shows the main street in Zyrardon. Nearly all the houses are built of wood, the streets are wretchedly kept, the horses are miserable-looking creatures, and the carts very primitive indeed. As is usual in all Polish towns, the Russian police are very much in evidence."

DRAWN BY HELEN McKIE

Helen McKie

Alongside the numerous artworks having on the walls of The Pheasantry Club were a series of London scenes by studio resident, Helen McKie. She painted murals of the Ritz's Rivoli Bar, and several of Butlin's holiday camps. She was an illustrator for The Bystander, and became well known for her drawings of military figures.

McKie gained remarkable access to two of the most important figures of the Second World War, Hitler and Churchill.

In 1931 she was admitted into the Nazi Party headquarters to sketch the Brown House, on the strength of a letter of introduction to Hitler.

Inside the album of 17 chilling drawings, McKie noted: *'Sketched in Hitler's Brown House Munich by special permission of Hitler's aide-de-camp Bruelenen - I was the only woman ever allowed to sketch here.'*

In 1943 she painted Sir Winston Churchill in the Upper War Room at Admiralty, Whitehall.

She is perhaps best remembered for her paintings of Waterloo station at war and at peace, commissioned by Southern Railway.

WATERLOO STATION

1848 — A CENTENARY OF UNINTERRUPTED SERVICE DURING WAR AND PEACE — 1948

SOUTHERN RAILWAY

WATERLOO STATION

1848 — A CENTENARY OF UNINTERRUPTED SERVICE DURING PEACE AND WAR — 1948

SOUTHERN RAILWAY

Writer Laurie Lee, by Ida Kar, 1956, ©National Portrait Gallery

Laurie Lee

Excerpt from *'Chelsea Towards the End of the Last War'* from *'Village Christmas: And Other Notes'* by *'Cider with Rosie'* author, Laurie Lee:

'Chelsea was seedy, calm and semi rustic at the time, with the charm of old paint and large undusted houses…

Chromium, Coca- Cola and cannabis had not yet touched the King's Road; in many ways it resembled a provincial high street of last century, full of tea shops, greengrocers and family butchers, though the butchers' windows showed only cardboard cut- outs of sheep…

There were really not many people about at the time a number of old activists, war artists and camouflage painters, the widows of artists and vivid ex- models, squeezing out their monthly bottle of gin…

For a treat I used to take my girls to the café across the road from The Markham Arms… Their kippers were the best I've ever known. Was that the last genuine eating house in Chelsea, I wonder, before the whole place fell to pizzas? The Pheasantry was another restaurant where you could dine for five shillings.

Imagine Chelsea as it was, with no cars parked in the street. The long mellow vista of terrace houses with their pavements running smooth and uncluttered, the streets wider and clear to the eye as they were designed to be…

After sundown there were no lights in streets or houses and the primeval darkness came back to London, a darkness which cleared the sky of its raw, neon- flecked glow and returned the sight of starts and the moon to the city. Flower- seeds blew in and thrived on the bomb sites and owls sang in the midnight blue. It was a time of strange peace that the war had given'.

From a selection of previously unknown essays found by his daughter Jessy Lee, and first published in 2015.

In the heart of Chelsea, so often and so wrongly called London's 'Montmartre'—for nothing could be less like the very English Bohemia in and around the King's Road. René, first proprietor, opened the Pheasantry here in the heart of Chelsea long before the last war. The food is very good and the price reasonable. Dancing to an accordion and a guitar is an accepted feature.

LONDON
NIGHT AND DAY

illustrated by

OSBERT LANCASTER

a guide to where the other books don't take you

THE 1950's

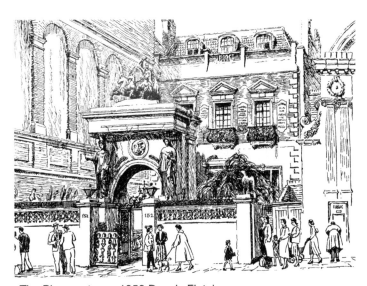

The Pheasantry, c. 1950 Dennis Fletcher

Chelsea is naughty. Chelsea is where artists live. And what is worse, it is where artists' models live. These two groups, of course, inevitably get together and the result is a hideous and incessant revel.

" any Londoner" an Englishman recently remarked, " can tell instantly that he's in Chelsea. All he has to do is look at the hats that people are wearing. In Mayfair or Victoria they would be wearing Homburgs. In the City, bowlers. But if you see a man wearing a paper bag, or a Swiss yodeler's hat or maybe a red stocking, then you know that you're in Chelsea".

He might have added that it is not even necessary to look for hats. if you see a girl wearing slacks it is absolutely impossible ha you are anywhere but in Chelsea. The souls are freer there.

Holiday Magazine, 1951

Inside The Pheasantry Club July 1950, ©Alamy

'After the pub crawl (the pubs close at 2 p.m.) the Chelsea-ites go off to lunch, and often they go to a fantastic club in the King's Road called the Pheasantry. This is not a pub, but a membership club, but since everyone belongs to it, the Pheasantry is almost a communal institution. It is in an old building (Henry VIII is supposed to have caroused here in his day) with a huge pillared entryway. Upstairs are studios and apartments; downstairs is the bar, restaurant and dance floor'.

Holiday Magazine, 1951

Above: Humphrey Bogart and Lauren Bacall were Pheasantry regulars and legend has it he proposed to his leading lady, who was 25 years his junior, at The Pheasantry Club.

Opposite page: Peter Ustinov met Suzanne Cloutier at The Pheasantry Club and the couple were married in Chelsea Register Office in 1954.

Peter Ustinov met Suzanne

THE PHEASANTRY

in Chelsea

152 KING'S ROAD,

MARIO will be pleased to

anytime, 12—3, 5—midnigh

Club is licensed, and you m

dine and dance any or e

Etching after Pietro Annigoni's 1955 portrait of Queen Elizabeth II

Pietro Annigoni

By 1955 painter Pietro Annigoni was holding court at The Pheasantry Club and living upstairs with the owner, René de Meo.

At this time Annigoni was working nearby in the studio of his pupil, Tim Whidborne, where he was finishing his 1955 portrait of Queen Elizabeth II.

He gave many works of art to the De Meos, including sketches drawn on the back of Pheasantry club menus which hung on the Pheasantry Club walls.

The Pheasantry's Pietro Annigoni admires his 1956 portrait of Dame Margot Fonteyn, who trained in Astafieva's Russian Dance Academy at The Pheasantry as a young dancer.

Some of the many art works by Pietro Annigoni given to The Pheasantry Club to cover his bills-

Sketch of a theatre, dedicated to Mario Cazzani, Pheasantry Club

"René had a heart attack once, thinking his collection of Annigoni sketches on the backs of menus had been stolen.

Annigoni, being very generous usually invited several friends, models and students to enjoy his hospitality with wine flowing and amusing conversation. Once, at the end of a two month visit to England, the bill presented was rather massive, but by painting Mario Cazzani's portrait the bill was cleared in full."

Annigoni, Village Church Sold at Christies. Provenance: Mario Cazzani, Pheasantry Club

114

PHEASANTRY CLUB

Menu

Saumon d'Ecosse Fumé 5/6   Potted Shrimps 4/-
Salami 3/6   Grape Fruit 2/-   Melon 2/6   Paté Maison 3/6

★

Minestrone 2/-   Crème de Tomate 2/-   Crème St. Jermain 2/-   Consommé 1/6

★

Spaghetti Bolognaise ou Napolitaine 3/6   Ravioli 4/-   Oeuf Brouilli Varie 3/6
Oeuf au Plat 2/6   Oeuf au Jambon 4/-   Oeuf au Lard 3/6   Omelette Maison 4/6
Omelette Varié 4/6   Sole Meunière 5/-   Sole Bonne Femme 5/6   Sole Maison 5/-
Homard Sur Comande

★

Specialite De La Maison

Shachlick 7/6   Steak Diane 6/6   Poulet Chasseur 6/6

★

Grouse   Perdreau   Faisan   Caneton   Poussin   Poulet Rôti
Suprême de Volaille Maison 7/-   Suprême de Volaille Poché au Riz Sauce Supreme 7/-
Poulet Grillé Américaine 7/6   Vol-au-Vent Regiane 5/6   Pilaff de Volaille 5/6
Entrecôte Grillé 7/-   Escalope de Veau Milanaise 7/-   Côtelette d'Agneau Grillé 5/6
Rognon Sauté 4/6   Goulash Hongroise 5/-   Foie de Veau Sauté 4/6
Foie de Volaille Livornaise 4/6   Jambon Sauce Madère 6/-
Côte de Porc Frais Grillé 6/-   Curry Madras 5/6

★

Pommes Sautés 1/-   Pommes Frites 1/-   Pommes Purée 1/-   Haricots Verts 1/6
Petits Pois 1/6   Chouxfleur 1/3   Epinard en Branche 1/3   Epinard à la Crème 1/6
Broccoli 1/9   Choux de Bruxelles 1/3   Celeri Braisé 1/6   Champignons Grillés 2/6

★

Crêpe Suzette 5/6   Omelette au Rhum 5/-   Glace Panaché 1/6   Méringue Glacée 2/-
Salade de Fruit Frais 2/-   Ananas a l'Orange 4/-   Pâtisserie 1/6   Zabalione 4/-
Soufflé au Grand Marnier 6/-

★

Welsh Rarebit 2/6   Champignons sur Toast 2/6   Sardines sur Toast 2/-
Canapé Diane 3/6

Club owner René De Meo collected a large number of drawings made on the backs of Pheasantry menus from his patrons, including these by Pietro Annigoni.

115

Author, Doris Lessing at The Pheasantry Club, 14 October 1957, for the launch of 'Declaration' a collaborative book of essays with Colin Wilson, John Osborne, John Wain, Kenneth Tynan, Lindsay Anderson and Stuart Holroyd. Below: the writers pose in the courtyard behind Joubert's fountain. ©Mirrorpix

Aneurin Bevan and Doris Lessing inside the Pheasantry in October 1957.

Aneurin Bevan

The Pheasantry Club didn't only attract artists, it was also a favourite haunt of politicians. Aneurin (Nye) Bevan, the chief architect of the NHS, was a frequent visitor and good friend of the Pheasantry Club owner, Rene de Meo. Being an Italian National, De Meo was interned as an enemy alien during the Second World War. The day after his release, he invited Bevan and his wife to dine with him in his flat at The Pheasantry.

In the post war years when rationing was still in place, Nye Bevan and his wife, the Labour MP Jennie Lee were dined with De Meo 'several times a week' according to his former mistress, Joan Parsons.

'If the ration weary public had discovered that two of the most vociferous advocates of 'fair shares for all', were fasting in public and feasting in private, the fragile support for post war austerity might have been shattered and with it the careers of Jennie Lee and Nye Bevan'.

Dr Mark Roodhouse, History Today 2005.

Dr Roodhouse recently discovered police interviews with De Meo and Joan Parsons in the National Archives. These were part of the 1948 Lynskey Tribunal, established to investigate corruption by leading government officials. Bevan was accused of black market deals by helping De Meo import furniture from Italy.

The Attorney-General in charge of the investigation decided that the allegations against Nye Bevan and Jennie Lee did not fall within the remit of the tribunal and the police took no further action.

Italian film star Rossano Brazzi, who played Emile De Becque in South Pacific, 'takes over the kitchen at the exclusive Pheasantry Club' with Elena Giusti, his wife, and Mario Cazzani. 1956.

Mario Cazzani

In 1958, following a heart attack, René De Meo retired to Italy, handing over the running of the club to Mario Cazzani who had already worked alongside him for many years.

During the war years Mario Cazzani was interned and was one of the survivors of the torpedoed Arandora Star, the boat that was carrying German and Italian internees. He did not, however, escape six weeks in prison for using butter and sugar in excess of rationing allowances for the restaurant.

Mario continued to run the Pheasantry Club until his sudden death in 1966.

Mario Cazzani poses at The Pheasantry bar with with his portrait and it's sculptor, Tony Gray.

When I ventured out with Carol it was to a different world. She used to frequent a club on the Kings Road called 'The Pheasantry'. It was very posh and very trendy. It was the combination of theatrical and posh that was so overwhelming to me...

The highlight of this period was Anthony Hopkins. He was going through a very difficult period in his life and was drinking heavily. He used to hold court at The Pheasantry doing his impersonation of Richard Burton doing Dylan Thomas.

I used to sit cross-legged on the floor in front of him, just listening. One night he noticed me, and we started  *talking and this was the cue for Carol to interrupt and drag me away'.*

Linda Bellingham, *'Lost and Found'*.

Into the 1960's...

Cartoon of The Pheasantry, c. 1960 unknown artist

IT'S DUD AND PETE . . . IN GEAR

Afraid of Virginia ? Sample line: "And : Bell told me about that ic pass you made at her at the fairy-ring last mmer's Eve. When you her back here to see 1st. She laughed so much oke her bell and couldn't tinkle for six months." Dudley was the mean, moody Melisande and Peter her longsuffering husband. The Royal Albert Hall was packed for the gala show, which raised nearly £2,000 for Oxfam. Among the stars who gave their time to perform for a good cause were the Alberts, Eleanor Bron, the Alan Price Set, Peter and Gordon, Jackie Trent, Paul Jones and Jeremy Taylor. After the show, stars and audience wound up at a party in the Pheasantry Club, Chelsea, which swung into the small hours.

'Pete and Dud' (Peter Cooke and Dudley Moore) and the cast of Oxfam's 'You're Joking Show' head to The Pheasantry where they partied into the early hours. Tatler, 24 December 1966.

Club advert, September 1965

The Pheasantry

There are so many changes in Chelsea these days. Vast glass and concrete monsters are sprouting in place of sedate town houses. There is a vast 'improvement scheme' in the offing. Not many years ago, you could count the number of restaurants on one hand; now their number has grown astonishingly.

But one thing that doesn't change with the years is the fascinating, utterly unique Pheasantry Club, at 152 King's Road.

The premises are in a building that was originally the hunting lodge of King Charles II. One story goes that it was a chief trysting place with Nell Gwynn! Even if this is doubtful, it's one of those legends one very much hopes is true.

Inside, you'll find a bar decorated with superb opulence. The mirrors are extravagantly gilded. On the walls are advertisements from the 20's and photographs of famous visitors who have patronised the Pheasantry.

Here, over the years, have met the really big names of intellectual London- Augustus John used to sit drinking with his models. Annigoni is a frequent visitor when he is in town.

Peter Ustinov proposed to his wife here. Merle Oberon never fails to drop in if she's making a film in Britain. The late Barok was a 'regular'.

For many years the Pheasantry has been under the control of expansive, amiable Mario Cazzani, who knows everyone and who must be just about the gayest host in London.

In the restaurant can be found paintings by many local artists. There's plenty of room for dancing, too. Life at the Pheasantry is apt to start late, the place really hots up around midnight.

All in all, the Pheasantry exudes the sort of atmosphere which I can only describe as being a skilful mixture of Edwardian and post-First World War. Bohemian it certainly is, but Bohemian with panache and sparkle.

Before I get down to the serious business of conveying the delights of the menu, let me stress that the Pheasantry is a club. In other words you have to be a member. This costs just one guinea a year. If you live in Britain Mario likes you to be introduced by another member, but is you're a visitor to these shores, you'll be welcomed during the period of your stay.

Take it from us, the Pheasantry is great fun. It has flourished in Chelsea for a great many years. I see no reason why it shouldn't stand until the day of judgement.

Patrick Richards

Review from What's On magazine, August 1964

THE PARTY'S OVER 'x' *Starring* Oliver REED · Clifford DAVID · Ann LYNN
Catherine WOODVILLE · Louise SOREL · Eddie ALBERT
A TRICASTLE PRODUCTION Released by MONARCH

Poster and scenes showing the exterior, the
the studios, and entranceway, with Oliver
Reed and Louise Sorel, from 'The Party's
Over' 1963

In 1963 The Pheasantry was once again became a film location. 'Party's Over' was written by Marc Behm, who also wrote the screenplay of The Beatles, 'Help! and 'Charade'. It was directed by Guy Hamilton who turned down 'Dr No' to direct this feature and would go on to direct 'Goldfinger' in 1964.

Future Bond film composer, John Barry provided the score. Yet when the film was deemed "Unpleasant, tasteless and rather offensive" by The British Board of Film Classification, the film was censored. Hamilton removed his name from the credits, and the release was delayed by a two year battle with censors. Largely filmed on location at the Pheasantry, it offers a glimpse of the house's interior including the studios, see opposite.

Interiors from the sketchbook of Birgitta Bjerke, Courtesy B. Bjerke

The Pheasantry goes Psychedelic

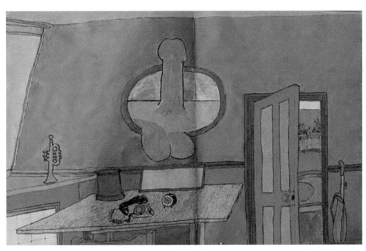

Interiors from the sketchbook of Birgitta Bjerke, Courtesy B. Bjerke

Upstairs...

Courtesy Bergitta Bjerke

One of several drawings made in a small notebook by artist and designer, Birgitta Bjerke, who stayed at The Pheasantry during the late 60's and early 70's.

A glimpse of the red and gilt of Sharp, Clapton and Mora's rooms in as they appeared in 1970 for The Italian Domus Magazine of Art and Architecture,

In the late 1960s The Pheasantry was a place of extraordinary creative activity and collaboration.

In 1967 Australian Martin Sharp and Eric Clapton moved in to a flat which they shared with Australian film maker, Philip Mora and photographer Robert Whittaker. Martin and Eric were soon joined by their girlfriends, the models and artists, Charlotte Martin and Eija Veka Aho.

The writer, cartoonist and art critic, Anthony Haden Guest had a flat there, Vogue photographer, Claude Virgin, a photography studio. Germaine Greer had a flat where she was writing 'The Female Eunuch'.

Eric Clapton and Charlotte Martin by Robert Whitaker, 1967 © Getty Images

Eric Clapton

'I had moved ... to the King's Road, Chelsea, to share a studio with Martin Sharp, with whom I had become good friends...Martin was ..an admirer of Max Ernst, who inspired a lot of his work, he was and still is a great painter.

...Our apartments on the top floor of The Pheasantry... We had a large kitchen, two or three bedrooms, and a huge living room with beautiful wooden floors and great views from the dormer windows. I decorated my room in bright red and gilt, a reflection of the times.'

Eric Clapton, *The Autobiography.*

'Eric asked me to design the cover for "Disraeli Gears". I loved record cover art and was very happy to do it. I commissioned my ex-studio mate, Bob Whitaker, to take some photos which were used in a collage on the back cover. I believe the photo used on the cover was a publicity shot that I got from Eric. I was using fluorescent paints at the time. It was the height of psychedelia.

Some of the ingredients in the cover are made up from Victorian decorative engravings. It was done in black and white first and then painted with fluorescent colours. I tried to capture the warm joyful liveliness of Cream's songs'.

Martin Sharp

'I was very lucky that Martin had discovered day-glo paint. I had all the pictures, which I knew were for some form of publicity. I made a whole series of colour prints and Martin just started cutting them up – much to my annoyance, because they weren't cheap to do. He then laid them out on a 12-inch square as a piece of finished artwork and then painted all over it'.

Photographer, Robert Whitaker

'Want to know what the 60s were like? Then look at Martin Sharp's work. .... Everybody who can remember anything about the 60s can remember Martin's poster of Dylan as Mr Tambourine Man, printed in red and black on gold paper'

Germaine Greer, 2009.

Poster by Martin Sharp and Vehka Aho,1966

Martin Sharp and Eija Veko Aho collaborated on the poster of Bob Dylan. She added the circles to the design but is not often credited.

'This poster is one of my first published works after my arrival in London in 1966. I can remember my dear friend Eija Vehka-aho creating all the beautiful circles that make up Bob Dylan's hair and which contribute so much to the work. The photograph, which forms the main image, was enlarged from a small photo in a book. The central image in the hair is a knot design, possibly by Leonardo da Vinci. Aubrey Beardsley's work was enjoying a revival at the time and there were many posters being produced from many sources and periods, as well as by the young artists of the day. There is certainly a Beardsley flavour. The lettering is by me and all these elements were collaged together to make the complete image. Bob Dylan's Mister Tambourine Man was a favourite song of mine. My poster is really just a tribute to Bob Dylan, a songwriter and singer I have greatly admired since first hearing him in 1964. The poster was printed by Peter Ledeboer, who was the printer of OZ Magazine, and he also distributed it to the numerous poster shops and stalls. It was sold for £1, in an unlimited edition, and was very much a part of the times in London in the late 1960s: a decoration'.

Martin Sharp quoted in 'Mister Tambourine Man', 2002.

Sharp used his image of Dylan as Mr Tambourine Man for the October 1967 cover of OZ

'I won't name drop, but it was astonishing the amount of different faces that would drop in throughout the course of the afternoon, and our 'tea parties' invariably evolved into whole evenings listening to music. Whether that might be the first pirated disc of Dylan's basement tapes, which I remember Litvinoff producing, or an acetate of a new Beetles song, or just me sitting in the corner playing guitar, there was always something going on'.

Eric Clapton, 'Autobiography'.

Kee and Ferrier on the cover of OZ, December 1968

"Australians seemed to be everywhere - moving and shaking in fine arts, music, theatre, in conventional, avant-garde and counter culture. I am not sure that such a combined outburst of Australian creativity hitting foreign shores has occurred since. Certainly it has not been properly documented since. Outsiders in London and expatriates from Australia, this intrepid group, as a group phenomenon, has fallen between the cracks for historians of culture ..."

Philippe Mora

Germaine Greer and Vivian Stanshall, Oz, March 1969.

Oz magazine, one of the most important underground counter-culture magazines was produced in London by Martin Sharp, Richard Neville and Jim Anderson. It also had contributions from Pheasantry residents Germaine Greer and Philippe Mora.

It challenged established norms tackling issues around feminism, the Vietnam war, racism, the pill, acid and more. The 1970 school kids issue led to the longest obscenity trial in British history, when it was charged with 'conspiracy to corrupt public morals", John Lennon and Yoko Ono joined protests and the charges were eventually dropped.

The FEMALE EUNUCH

Germaine Greer

in Philippe Mora's film 'Darling ,do you love me?', 1968

Germaine Greer

'Germaine Greer starred as a chanteuse in my first feature film, Trouble in Molopolis, made in 1969. She lived downstairs from me in London. I was in awe of her.

At that time, 'The Female Eunuch' was yet to be published. She was a comedic actress and singer, doing things for the BBC. She could have had a great career if she wanted to do that'.

Philippe Mora, Sydney Morning Herald, 2016.

Mora and John Ivor Greenwood, introduced to Mora
by David Litvinov, in in Trouble in Molopolis,

Poster by Martin Sharp and Philippe Mora
courtesy of Philippe Mora

Philippe Mora

Philippe Mora shot his first feature-length film 'Trouble In Molopolis' (1970) in The Pheasantry.
Financed by Arthur Boyd and Eric Clapton, Mora said the cast consisted of "every Australian I
knew"; Germaine Greer played a cabaret singer, Martin Sharp a mime and Richard Neville a PR
man. The lead actor was John Ivor Greenwood. a character introduced to Mora by David
Litvinoff, who he describes as "a real lunatic".

Trouble in Molopolis opened at the nearby Paris Pullman cinema in 1970 as a fundraiser for
OZ and was introduced by George Melly.

*"The festivities were only slightly delayed when the loony star defecated in the front row and
and then passed out in an alcoholic coma."* (Philippe Mora)

"Soon I ended up living with Martin Sharp and Eric Clapton in the Pheasantry on King's Road, a grand old building with a bohemian and artistic history... Our Pheasantry scene was a kind a kind of cultural catalyst and melting pot. R.D Laing would drop by and say we were normal and everyone else was crazy... Bob Whitaker, talented photographer, lived around the corner... Germaine Greer lived downstairs, working on a book. George Harrison would drop by..."

Philippe Mora

Philippe Mora in The Pheasantry 1970, with his painting 'Popeye and Olive's Expulsion from Paradise'. Used in 'The Beatles Illustrated Lyrics', the couple represent John and Yoko. Photographed at The Pheasantry by Angus Forbes. © Philippe Mora

George Harrison, 1967 © Alamy

George Harrison

'Life soon settled into the old routine, with people dropping in for test and musical soirées. A regular visitor was George Harrison, who I had known since we met when I was in the Yardbirds'.

Eric Clapton, *'The Autobiography'*

Litvinoff at The Pheasantry. Photos courtesy Mora, © Mora/Sharp

David Litvinoff

David Litvinoff grew up in the East end of London and was a fast-talking hard man, with an ear to ear scar etched across his face. He claimed it was "a little present from the Kray twins". Litvinoff had a flair for story telling and for exaggeration, but his links to the Krays *was* real. In 1858 Lucian Freud painted him as 'The Procurer', and their row over the painting's title made it into the headlines.

Litvinoff was a friend of the artist, Tim Whidborne, and worked part time as his secretary as he had done for Lucian Freud during the 1950's. He more or less lived at the Pheasantry, becoming close to Eric Clapton, who writes "He was absolutely extraordinary. I loved him to bits".

Litvinoff had a profound influence on the film 'Performance' in which Mick Jagger plays a reclusive pop star. The film's director, Donald Cammel, had appointed Litvinoff 'dialogue consultant' and 'technical advisor'. But he has been credited with many aspects of the film's power.

Litvinoff as 'The Procurer', by Pheasantry Club member, Lucian Freud.

'It was quite a community of people living in the Pheasantry. Martin and I had two of the rooms which we shared with our respective girlfriends Ejia and Charlotte. The third room was taken by another painter, Philippe Mora and his girlfriend Freya, and the ground floor was a massive studio owned or leased by a portrait painter named Tim Whidborne, who was busy painting the Queen's portrait, while we were upstairs quietly getting out of our skulls. But the most colourful character in our midst, if not the most powerful, was David Litvinoff'.

Eric Clapton, The Autobiography

'It was great to be back at The Pheasantry, where Litvinoff was in an excitable mood, having been employed as dialogue coach and technical advisor on a film, 'Performance', which was being shot in Chelsea by Donald Cammell and Nick Roeg...One night he brought around the director, Donald Cammell, who managed to stage a power cut in the flat, and then tried to grope my girlfriend Charlotte in the dark. A peculiar chap'.

Eric Clapton, *'The Autobiography'*

In a letter in 1968 he tells his friend that Mick Jagger is considering buying the studio from Tim Whidborne:

'I forgot to mention Tim was going to sell his studio to Mick Jagger and his lady love Miss Faithful and is hoping to recover all his bread which he has spent there over the past few years in this transaction. He doesn't really dig the place so much now, as the Pheasantry Club has been taken over by the Speakeasy club people, and this means he will have about a thousand hippies hovering around his door each night, so he wants to cool his own scene there'.

Litvinoff as quoted in *'Jumpin' Jack Flash'*, by Keiron Pim.

Tim Whidborne didn't hand his studio over to Mick Jagger, but stayed there while he was working on his portrait of Queen Elizabeth II in 1969.

Mick Jagger as Turner, in 'Performance', which captures the atmosphere of the 1960's and which Litvinov imbued with menace.

'The particular expertise for which he had been hired was his knowledge of the underworld, as the movie, which was basically a star vehicle for Mick Jagger playing a faded rock idol, was set in the world of London gangsters. He was full of ideas about how he felt the story should develop, and every day he would come and see me and tell me about all the goings on on set and to fill me in on whatever was going to happen the next day'.

Eric Clapton, *The Autobiography*

Annigoni's 1969 Portrait of the Queen. © National Portrait Gallery

Tim Whidborne in his Pheasantry Studio with his portrait of 'Queen Elizabeth II on horseback as Colonel in chief of the Irish Guards' at the Pheasantry. Courtesy Tim Whidborne, 1969. On the wall behind him is Annigoni's 1855 painting of The Queen and a portrait of The Duke of Edinburgh.

Tim Whidborne

A former pupil of Pietro Annigoni, Tim Whidborne shared his studio with his teacher while he was working on his first portrait of the Queen in 1955. By 1969 both teacher and pupil were working on royal portraits:

'While at least some of Whidborne's neighbours upstairs were experimenting with every type of weapons- grade narcotics they could get their hands on, the artist himself was hard at work on an official portrait of the Queen astride a horse called Doctor.'

Paul Scott, Motherless Child: The definitive Biography of Eric Clapton

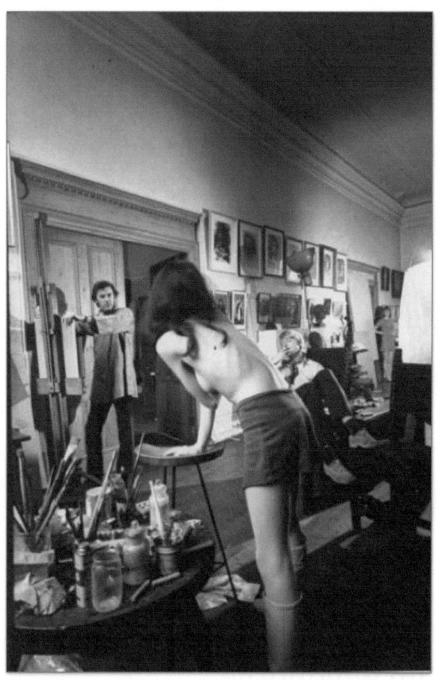

'I was fortunate to have stayed at The Pheasantry with Tim Whidborne and Annigoni.

Annigoni was painting the queen and there were lots of freehand sketches everywhere. The studio catered for several people, of which I was one.

The Pheasantry was like the Tardis and there were hundreds of rooms and studios with artists and photographers staying there'.

Richard Levesley, 'Into my veins'.

Tim Whidborne in Pheasantry 'studio 1', with novelist Adam Diment and Suzie Mandrake. Photo Loomis Dean

Tim Whidborne entertaining at The Pheasantry

Vogue Cover by Claude Virgin, 1 March, 1962

Claude Virgin

'I met Claude Virgin in the Bistro, a restaurant off Sloane Square, run by a warm-hearted tyrant, Elisabeth Furse, my mother. Virgin was an habitué. We became friendly and together took over a sprawling double studio behind the Pheasantry on the King's Road. It goes without saying that a photographer's fashion and beauty studio was not a horrible place for a young man - I was down from Cambridge - to be. And Claude Virgin was its most entertaining element.

The studio seating consisted mostly of Mies van de Rohe "Barcelona" chairs. The art included a supposed Rothko and Virgin's portrait, painted by a friend, Donald Cammell, but the principal wall adornment was a huge wooden aeroplane propeller'.

Anthony Haden-Guest

American born fashion photographer, Claude Virgin had a studio at The Pheasantry while he was working for British Vogue from 1957 and into the 60s. He was described by Helmut Newton as "sexy and different from anything seen before in England".

Birgitte Bjerke

Counter-culture designer Birgitta Bjerke, stayed at The Pheasantry at the tail end of this period filling a small black book with watercolour drawings of the interiors, (see opposite).

The fashion and costume designer's crochet's commissions included designs for Eric Clapton, coats for Roger Daltry (of The Who) and his wife. She also made a full length crochet gown and bedspread for Frankie Azzara, the singer who, in 1969, was going out with Grateful Dead guitarist, Bob Weir.

Birgitta Bjerke teaching Joni Mitchell to crochet!

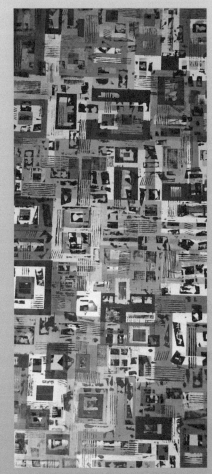

Painting by Charlotte Martin and image from c. 1967, courtesy C. Martin

Charlotte Martin

Model-turned-artist Charlotte Martin lived at The Pheasantry with Eric Clapton until 1968. She had a successful modelling career and was very much part of the swinging sixties pop scene, dating George Harrison for a time, and then Led Zeppelin's guitarist, Jimmy Page with whom she had a daughter.

"I was smitten with her from the very first moment I set eyes on her. She was very beautiful in an austere way, classically French, with long legs and an incredible figure, but it was her eyes that got on me. They were slightly Asian with a downward slant, and a little bit sad . . . Charlotte was an incredible girl, more interested in films, art and literature than in modelling, and we had a great time together."

Eric Clapton 'The Autobiography'

Jenny Kee's presence at the speakeasy attracted the patronage of Martin Sharp, the old dog. One night as they flirted over a drink order, the pair were introduced to the virtuoso guitarist from the supergroup Cream... Martin brought out a crumpled envelope.

'I've just written a song,' he announced, showing the guitarist his scribbled yearnings for a summer in Sydney and a spell with his absent heartthrob, Anou.

'That's great' replies Eric, another ex-art student, I've just written some music...

Sharp's heroic angst slotted with Clapton's bass guitar riffs. These two rising stars of psychedelia decided to share lodgings in the King's Road at The Pheasantry, the former home of Nell Gwynn, mistress of Charles II. Sharp executed a fluorescent cover for the next Cream LP, Disraeli Gears, and one of its finest tracks was Sharp's song, 'Tales of Brave Ulysses."

'*Hippie Hippie Shake*', Richard Neville.

' *I'd heard about Eric Clapton, of course. I'd seen th Graffiti (Clapton is God) on the wall outside th Pheasantry'. Chris O Dell.*

154

Jenny Kee wearing a costume from the 1914 Ballet Russes production of Le Coq d'Or designed by Natalia Goncharova. Etching after photograph by William Yang. The dress was a gift from Lambert, with whom she worked a the Chelsea Market.

Jenny Kee

Jenny Kee was working as a model at the time she was living at the Pheasantry and selling ethnic and vintage clothes at The Chelsea market, opposite the Pheasantry.

A self confessed groupie she was close to John Lennon, Eric Clapton, Keith Richards and Roger Daltry. She later recalled, "If you're going to be a groupie, well, I went to the top".

In 1972 she returned to Australia to open a fashion boutique. Today she is a celebrity designer thanks to her eclectic style and use of colour.

Meanwhile downstairs...

NOUGHT VERY COMFORTABLE

Portrait of the artist as a doodler. Henry Sutton, who wrote the best-selling novel "The Exhibitionist" daubs noughts and crosses on a topless model at a party held at the Pheasantry Club, King's Road, Chelsea to launch his book in this country.

On the cover of the book there is a back view of a psychedelically painted lady.

It's a change anyway from discreet literary luncheons.

K18

'The likelihood of having your drink spiked with acid was pretty high'.

In 1966 Pheasantry Club owner, Mario Cazzani died suddenly. His death marked the end of The Pheasantry Club, and the beginning of a new era in the building's basement and studios.

'There would be an R&B club for a bit, and then everybody would get fed up with the noise, or the parking or the cops or something , and then they'd become a gay club for a while, and there'd be Lindsay Kemp in there doing what Lindsay Kemp sort of did. The Pheasantry always seemed to be hosting various floating crap games, some of which were R &B, some of which were folk music and some of which were gay. I think they had a back room where the doors were closed and people went on drinking, and I think there were gangsters involved.'

Author, Barry Miles

While upstairs art and music were being created, down in the basement some of the biggest acts of the 1970's were getting their first break. It might have been considered a second rate venue, but The Pheasantry saw gigs by Thin Lizzy, Sparks, Queen, Lou Reed and Hawkwind. The 20 year old Andrew Lloyd Webber discovered 17 year old Yvonne Elliman singing here, who he cast in his early hit musical 'Jesus Christ Superstar'.

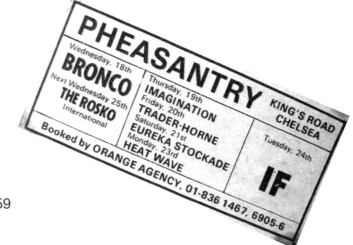

Thin Lizzy, 1972 © Alamy

Thin Lizzy

Guitarist Gary Moore recalled seeing Thin Lizzie perform there:

'I remember going to see them play at a place called The Pheasantry Club in the Kings Road and thinking how sad it was for Lizzy. They were just playing to a handful of posey people sitting there drinking cocktails, and the whole scenario just wasn't right'.

Queen in the early 1970's, ©Trinity Mirror/ Mirrorpix/ Alamy

Queen

In November 1972, two weeks after recording their first album 'Queen' at Trident Studios, the band put on a show case at The Pheasantry. They had hoped this gig would get them a record deal but the A&R people didn't show up...Phil Reed recalled:

'Not one A&R guy turned up. It was really a disco place and once the disco had stopped and Queen started went on everyone went to the bar. Once Queen started virtually everyone had left the room... There were only a few of the bands friends left'.

Phil Reed, as quoted in ''*Queen': The Early Years'* by Mark Hodgkinson.

They were, however, signed up by EMI just a few weeks later.

Sparks playing at The Pheasantry November 1972 © Photo Michael Putland/ Getty Images

Sparks

Sparks manager, John Hewlett was dismissive about the The Pheasantry:

'It was a naff place to play. It was the sort of place you played if you couldn't get the Marquee. It wasn't the greatest of gigs but then they weren't the greatest of bands and it was a gig. The main thing was them playing anywhere'.

Lou Reed, 1972 © Alamy

Lou Reed

On 2 November 1972 Lou Reed played The Pheasantry, shortly after recording his album 'Transformer' which featured 'Walk on the Wild Side' and 'Perfect Day'. It was produced by David Bowie and Mick Ronson, and was released 6 days after his Pheasantry gig.

John Newey and John Wight in Crew playing at The Pheasantry, 1971

The Pheasantry under Threat

While Eric Clapton was hosting his 'tea parties', Queen was performing in the basement and Tim Whidborne was painting his official portrait of the Queen, The Pheasantry was on borrowed time. Plans had been submitted to Kensington and Chelsea Council to completely demolish The Pheasantry and replace it with a 266 bedroom hotel and eighteen shops.

In 1969, Germaine Greer agreed, *"in its present state it isn't worth preserving"*. But suggested, *"The arts council or someone should take it over and turn it into art commune."* A group of local residents challenged the council, and had plans drawn up for an arts centre surrounded by gardens. These visions were soon squashed by developers.

In 1968 Tim Whidborne had arranged for a blue plaque to be erected for Princess Serafina Astafieva as an attempt to save at least part of the building from demolition. As he explained to me, *"I realised that a blue plaque on the façade would, or might be another reason to save the building from the threatened application to knock it down"*.

Mick Farren, (Germaine Greer's lover at the time), described the building:

"It was falling down. It had sort of gone through its popular phase, but no money had been put back into it to fix the roof and stuff, and the roofs were leaking and everything was kind of coming apart and Martin Sharp was moving in and all that was left behind were a few upper class junkies who couldn't move when the party moved on."

Eric Clapton left the Pheasantry in the late sixties soon after a legendary failed drugs bust, and the others were to follow. Birgitta Bjerke explained, "We left the Pheasantry after the police came and freaked everyone out". Artist Tim Whidborne's lease was not renewed, and soon the building stood empty.

The building started to crumble, at which point developers argued it wasn't worth saving.

It was too late to save The Classic, or 12 Jubilee place, which had now been torn down, but there was a massive backlash from the who recognised the cultural and historical significance of the Pheasantry.

The fight to save the Pheasantry from total demolition had begun.

When asked about their plans, the Cadogan Estate office told Hillier: "It is pretty tatty outside, and then you get inside, it's even more tatty. We feel it has come to the end of its useful life".

Saving The Pheasantry

'If architecture is frozen music, the Pheasantry in Kings Road, Chelsea must be the 'Ride of the Valkyries'. The great black stone horses tearing on the portico look as if they are about to start up their jet engines and carry the building shuddering into the shy. And surely the villainous beaky birds that flank the walls are Sinbad- type rocs, not silly pheasants. 'The Pheasantry' : what a profanely insipid bane for this perverted palace, which might be a chapel of Beelzebub, Alister Crowley's pied-à-terre, a crèche for Rosemary's baby or a finishing school for vampires.

There are plenty of rustic follies, mad pavilions on hilltops, blind gazebos and prefabricated ruins wrestling with the ivy. The Pheasantry is that far rarer and more inspired invention; the town folly. If I were editing I-Spy books, you would score 20 points for a fake hunting lodge or a dovecote that doubles as a summerhouse, and 100 points for the Pheasantry. To demolish it - and that is what a form of property speculators are planning at this moment would maim Chelsea horribly and I think mortally, by razing one landmark that can still lord it with style in that wilderness of boutiques and coffee bars. Without it, the King's Road would simply be another Carnaby Street, stretches to breaking point. If it does go, its epitaph might be an adaptation of Yeats most famous line: 'A terrible deputy is dead.'

Bevis Hiller, Harpers Magazine, 1969.

Future of the Pheasantry

From Sir John Betjeman and others

Sir, We would like to draw the attention of the residents of Kensington and Chelsea and all those who are interested in the past and future of this historic borough that the future of the Pheasantry site is to be decided on Tuesday, September 26, by the town planning committee. The plan submitted by Pearce & Co involves the construction of a tower block which will dwarf and darken the courtyard and façade of the Pheasantry, which is a listed building, Markham Street and Jubilee Place beside it.

An alternative scheme has been submitted which would offer to the borough an arts centre in a form more sympathetic to the environment at negligible cost to the ratepayer. The centre would be financed by the commercial side of the development. It is our hope that Standing Committee will consider these points.

Yours faithfully,
JOHN BETJEMAN,
ANGELA ANTRIM,
ELIZABETH LONGFORD,
DIONE GIBSON,
JULIAN JEBB,
14 Moore Street, SW3.
September 24.

John Betjeman's Letter to The Times, 26 September 1978

PREAMBLE

At the moment the Pheasantry, a Grade II Listed Building and, what is more, a well-known and well-loved landmark of the King's Road, is standing derelict and abandoned, a victim of the wind and the rain and of property developers' blight, in the midst of an area of rubble that resembles a bomb-site, shielded from the scandalized public view by garish wooden hoardings.

Yet only a few years ago it was a fine, lively place, an arts club patronized by such eminent artists as Annigoni and (to go back a little further) Augustus John; with the Chelsea Classic, so much a part of the younger generation's lives, on one side and a row of charming Victorian cottages, including a listed Gothic folly, No.12 Jubilee Place on the other. Now all these have been uselessly and wilfully demolished, leaving a desolation in thie place. Why? Basically to satisfy the greed of property-developers and land-owners - sacrifice to the golden idols of our over-commercialised society.

Yet amidst these ruins, this delapidation, this decay, hope like a fragile snowdrop blossoms anew. The ghastly mistakes of the last decade, of the get-rich-quick vandals, are not now likely to be repeated. Property developers and the large landlords are not less greedy; but they have become more bashful - and less likely to get credit at economic interest rates. And in the case of this particular site a wonderful opportunity has now fallen into Chelsea's lap - an opportunity here now, ready and waiting to be seized; the opportunity to restore the King's Road own little "palace", to clear up the site around it and to create there perhaps a garden - a green open space - in such a way that the Pheasantry will become an ornament to Chelsea and indeed to London, a source of pride to residents and a real attraction to tourists, by contrast with the more and more tawdry featured of the King's Road as it has now become.

The Future of The Pheasantry

Plans for The Pheasantry to be turned into a community centre for the arts September 1976

Years of protest against demolition and commercial redevelopment of the site of the Pheasantry began in 1969, with when proposals for the hotel and offices were first submitted to the council.   The council heeded and stipulated developers retain the facade, courtyard arch and Turret House at number 12 Jubilee Place. Plans were therefore revised to incorporate shops, flats and offices.

'The Friends of the Pheasantry' and a charity, 'The Pheasantry Arts Trust Association' was set up to pay for an alternative plan to be drawn up 'by those hoping to save the Pheasantry for community use'. But the plans for an arts centre, with children's theatre, cinema, writing and exhibition centre were rejected by Kensington and Chelsea council on the grounds they "failed to make best use of the land in the interests of the local community".

The Friends of the Pheasantry held open meetings, gathered support of many locals, celebrities and artists and published 'The Pheasantry Dossier', and John Betjeman wrote to The Times to appeal for an alternative plan for the building on the grounds of its cultural and architectural importance. But protests fell on deaf ears.

In 1972 listed building consent was given for the demolition of Joubert's Turret House on Jubilee Place by the same council inspector who had previously described it as 'a rare example of a Victorian period rendering of French mediaeval architecture'.

In 1973 The Classic Cinema was pulled down along with other neighbouring buildings belonging to the Pheasantry site.

By 1974 all that remained of The Pheasantry, Pheasantry Studios, Chelsea Classic and surrounding buildings was the Pheasantry's façade and entrance arch.

●The Pheasantry this week.
(Photo: David Ingham).

Pleasantry takes a tur

Behind the facade

One of the four gold horses on top of the P King's Road has taken a fall

Development of the site surrounding th (partly saved from demolition after a fight by now well advanced, and some observers thir have taken a tumble during building works legs.

Built by the French and designed by Joubert, the quadriga of horses are a copy of those outside the Louvre in Paris and are an important part of the central section of the Pheasantry, which is now subject to a preservation order.

No spokesman for the

builders, Pearce Brothers, was available at time of going to press.

A spokesman for The Friends of Chelsea said they would be investigating what damage, if any, had occurred to the horse, making sure that the horse is replaced in his rightful position as soon as possible.

The glory that has gone . . . a recent view of The Pheasantry, King's Road, erstwhile haunt of the famous.

Conditional on redevelopment has been retention of the facade: This rear view taken from Jubilee Place, by Chelsea News photographer David Ingham, indicates how the facade has been — as one apprehensive Chelsean has put it — "hanging on by the skin of it's teeth."

NOW NEARING completion, The Pheasantry in King's Road is beginning to look familiar again as the famous archway with its quadriga and caryatids are unveiled.

Unfortunately, however, the builders appear to have been a little too enthusiastic with their paint and brushes — having covered the two Greek ladies with white paint after the restorers had painstakingly managed to achieve a perfect bronze - looking finish at their studios in Glebe Place!

But despite this unfortunate 'cover - up', applications for the future use of the building are now coming in fast. They include an application for a restaurant, coupled with a conservatory extension, as well as plans for a hair - dressing salon.

The restaurant, it seems, is the idea of Trevor Davies who hopes to open in December after spending £500,000 on equipping it, according to recent reports. He will be following a distinguished tradition which was dominated by Alex Stirling's famous venue in the fifties.

"We want to keep the artistic feel it had in the fifties when Annigoni and Prince Philip used to come here," Mr. Davies says.

Above The King's Road showing The Pheasantry, c. 1970, below c. 1990.

1980, Toad Hall and the Pheasant Pluckers

After more than ten years of plans, negotiations, fights and construction The Pheasantry reopened in the early 1980s. Painted gaudy colours by new owners in 1984 it briefly changed its name to 'Toad Hall' though that didn't last long…

Chelsea Colours

'Toad Hall (formerly known as The Pheasantry), the cocktail bar and club on the King's Road, has recently had a complete refurbishment. Owner Gary Caesar is delighted with the redesign, which includes a startling new frontage, intended to appeal to the youth market. The building's distinctive 30' archway with its pillars has metamorphosed from plain white to a rainbow of colours. 'It's such a beautiful building and the new colours make it a real feature', said Cathy Ashley of Absolute Interiors, the company responsible for the design. However, a group of local Chelsea residents think that Toad Hall now looks more like a bad LSD trip, and have launched a campaign to get the building all white again. Number 152 King's Road is in fact a listed building, dating from 1850, and noted as being a 'curiosity' with its stucco and iron balconies'.

Jane Bartlet, The Times 13/1/84

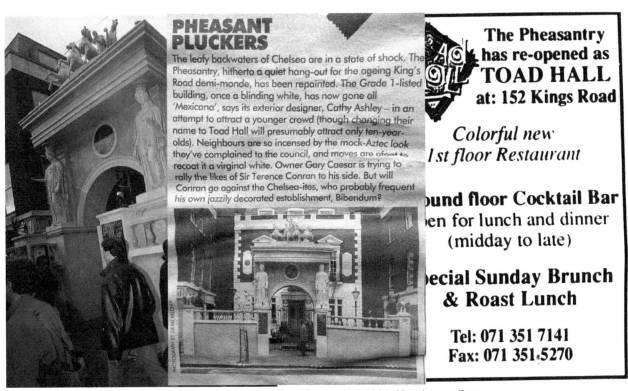

Evening standard magazine 30/9/1984 and advert from 3 November 1984, Kensington Post

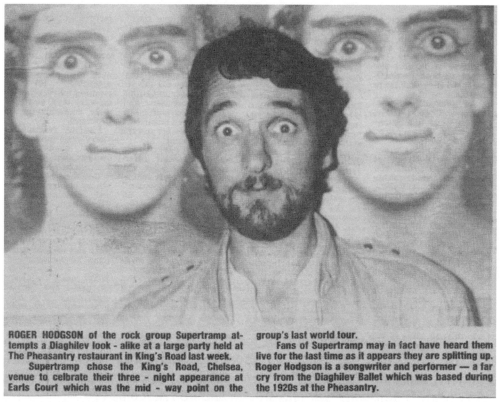

ROGER HODGSON of the rock group Supertramp attempts a Diaghilev look - alike at a large party held at The Pheasantry restaurant in King's Road last week.

Supertramp chose the King's Road, Chelsea, venue to celbrate their three - night appearance at Earls Court which was the mid - way point on the group's last world tour.

Fans of Supertramp may in fact have heard them live for the last time as it appears they are splitting up. Roger Hodgson is a songwriter and performer — a far cry from the Diaghilev Ballet which was based during the 1920s at the Pheasantry.

Supertramp's Rodger Hodgson as Diaghilev at a party at The Pheasantry, 1983. Below: The Cast of Jukebox the Musical celebrate opening at The Pheasantry also in 1983

1990... Ray Camino

The building continued to change hands names and guises; it was sold on in 1987 for £7 million and continued to morph. The basement was turned into a Spanish tapas bar 'Ray Camino' in 1990... and upstairs, where Astafieva once taught her pupils, and before that Nicholson painted his mistress, there was a fish and chip shop or 'chic chippie'

Exotic animals return to the Pheasantry for the opening the Pheasantry as Rey Camino in April 1990. I'm sure Samuel Baker would have been delighted, as, no doubt would Luisa Casati who collected a menagerie of wild animals as pets. But in these post - imperial days, the stunt proved uncomfortable with some of the guests including Bob Geldof, Alison Doody, and what the evening standard described a 'a brace of Penthouse models'...

Cleo Rocos riding an elephant at the opening of 'Ray Camino' at The Pheasantry in April 1990.

'Above the hum of Rioja- inspired fashion banter, a clutch of animal lovers were expressing concern that Rosa might not be entirely happy, a view strongly denied by the City of London divisional vet.

But Rosa showed no objection when Annabelle Heseltine, daughter of Michael, was coaxed onto her back for the benefit of the assembled paparazzi'.

It is downstairs where the change is noticeable. Where late-nighters once propped up the bar by a tiny dance floor and smooching couples sought out dark corners, now flamenco and lambada dancers set the pace. San Miguel has taken the place of pina colada.

Music returns to The Pheasantry

Getting ready for one of my shows at The Pheasantry

The Pheasantry basement today.   Kerry Ellis, with Music Manager, Ross Dines and Brian May

In 2010 London lost one of its most important jazz and cabaret venues, 'Pizza on the Park'. Westminster council had approved plans and given the go ahead for change of use into a luxury hotel. By the time jazz and cabaret fans had heard about it, it was too late.

Over three decades the cherished venue, with its arched windows and traditional red tiled facade (reminders of its former life as an underground station), saw jazz and theatrical mega stars perform here including George Melly, Barbara Cook, Blossom Dearie, Mose Allison, Clare Martin, John Dankworth and Cleo Lane, Barb Jungr, to name but a few.

Queen's guitarist, Brian May, returns to The Pheasantry in 2016 Photo Ross Dines

Pizza Express Music manager, Ross Dines, took the grand piano, sound equipment and staff from the basement of Pizza on the Park and installed them into the basement of The Pheasantry. And a new jazz-cabaret venue was born.

In the last ten years as a major music venue, The Pheasantry has attracted some of the finest jazz and cabaret artists and musicians. In good Pheasantry tradition, it hosts many young and up-and-coming acts, as well as established names including Liane Carroll, Claire Martin, John Etheridge, Barb Jungr, Anne Reid, Nicky Haslam, Elaine Delmar, Dillie Keane, Peter Atkin, John Standing, and in 2016 Queen's Brain May returned to the basement.

Liane Carroll and Gwilym Simcock, photographer unknown.

Clarke Peters, © Tatiana Gorilovsky

Joanna Strand singing with Ann Hampton Calloway, © K.Strand

Cleo Higgins © Ross Dines

Clare Teal © Ravi Chandarana

Michelle Brouerman © Ravi Chandarana

Deva Mahal, © Rosa Jorba

Anne Reid © MEP

John Standing photographer unknown

Joanna Strand © Tim Motion

The Pheasantry today

It is fitting that The Pheasantry is now a music venue-for it has resonated with music for decades. Our eccentric polymath, Felix Joubert, composed for the piano here, meanwhile upstairs, you could hear the sound of Serafina Astafieva's pianist as they played for classes in Studio 1.

Felix Joubert 'Romance Pour Piano'

Her former pupil, Sir Anton Dolin remembers:

'Sometimes we had no pianist, and then she would sing or chant in a rich, typically Russian voice, and beat time with her stick. (Dolin, Ballet- Go -Round)'.

There were dance bands in the 1940's, which Nicolette Devas recalled *almost* blocked out the sounds of war:

'The place was crammed; I was not the only one who wanted to forget the danger. A bomb had cut the electricity and René, the proprietor, lit a few candles, in short supply like everything else. The guns from Battersea Park barked over the roof and the whine and thump of bombs sounded all round with the ominous drone of enemy planes. The dance music worked hard against the air- raid noises, but that night it failed to blot them out'.

In the 1950's, you might catch an impromptu performance by the Italian operatic tenor, Beniamino Gigli or Luigi Infantino, encouraged by René de Meo. René himself had once hoped to be a singer, and acted as the London agent for the great Infantino. Or perhaps you would hear a song from his wife, Pamela, who was a trained pianist, and sang in five languages.

By 1965 June Fraser and Marylin Eliot's guitar and accordion duo had been entertaining club patrons for more than 8 years. Alistair Revie, from the Kensington Post wrote:

'Yes, I said girls. It's the only night club I know in the world with a girlie music group in residence. They are, of course, first rate musicians…'

He also noted that:

'It's not unusual for a dozen stars from the Covent Garden opera to be in the club, filling the ballroom with spontaneous song'.

During the 1970's, in the squalor of the basement, an extraordinary array of rising stars performed. Upstairs, Eric Clapton played his guitar, or jammed with George Harrison in his top floor flat.

And so, I leave this building, and this history in the same way as I found it; through music.

If walls could speak…I wonder, with all the secrets they have kept; the loves, the crimes; the art, and for all the ecstasy, misery and creativity, perhaps these walls wouldn't speak. These walls would sing.

Joanna Strand, London, September 2019.

Acknowledgements

Thanks to my exceptional daughters for their enthusiasm and positivity, and to Simon, for his wisdom and support.

Thanks to Michael and Linda Bell for all their warmth and passion for my project, and all the information about and photographs of grandfather, Felix Joubert.

To Timothy Whidborne for his letters and stories, and indeed for being a major part of the fight to save the Pheasantry from demolition in the 70's, and for his restoration of the archway!

Thanks also to Charlotte Martin and to Birgitta Bjerke for your contributions and sharing your recollections of the haze of those psychedelic years. Philippe Mora too for your memories and encouragement and all the photographs.

Thanks to Desmond Banks for advice and kind permission to print Sir William Nicholson's work.

Thanks to René and Pamela's son Justin De Meo and to Howard Phillips, grandson of Charles Sykes for their invaluable recollections.

Thanks to the team at The British Library especially for bringing out the tomes that are Joubert's illustrated guide to Arms and Armour. To Kensington and Chelsea Library, for lugging trolly loads of rate books and maps and copies of The Chelsea Times. Thanks especially to Dave Walker for sharing photographs and his wealth of knowledge. To the librarians at the Victoria and Albert Museum Archive for access to Anton Dolin's personal scrapbooks.

And a massive thank you to Ross Dines at Pizza Express for your support, and for commissioning this history of an amazing building. And indeed -for the opportunity to perform regularly at this wonderful venue- it is always a joy.

Bibliography

Anderson, Clive, (2008) *Politically Charged, The Oz Trial*. BBC. Anderson, Jim (2011). *Lampoon: An Historical Art Trajectory 1970/2010.* Dennis Publishing.

Annigoni, Pietro (1977) An Autobiography W.H. Allen London Bellingham, Lynda (2011). Lost and Found: My Story. London: Ebury Press.

Brown, Mick, *Sex-crazed Rupert the Bear and other stories... The obscenity trial that brought down Oz magazine*, The Daily Telegraph, London, 28 July 2017

Browse, L., (1956) *William Nicholson*, London.

Cadogan, Patrick (2008). *The Revolutionary Artist: John Lennon's Radical Years*. Lulu.

Cammell, Charles (1956) Memoirs of annigoni Allan Wingate publishers London

Campbell, C. (1992) *William Nicholson: The Graphic Work*, London

Campbell, James, Reed and Schwartz, (2005) The art of William Nicholson, Royal Academy of Arts

Carpenter, Humphrey (1988*) A Serious Character: The Life of Ezra Pound*, Orion Hardbacks

Carroll, Mark (2011*). The Ballets Russes in Australia and Beyond*. Wakefield.

Clapton Eric (2008) *The Autobiography* Arrow books London

Commedia/Banks, (1995) *William Nicholson: Landscape and Still Life*, Eastbourne

Croot, Patricia (Editor), (2004) *Economic history: Trade and industry in A History of the County of Middlesex: Volume 12: Chelsea*. www.british-history.ac.uk.

Darwin Correspondence Project, (2019) University of Cambridge.

David Buckman (2006). *Artists in Britain Since 1945 Vol 2, M to Z.* Art Dictionaries Ltd

Davidson, Andrew (9 September 1995*). "The old devil"*. The Independent.

Decharne, Max. (2005) *King's Road: The Rise and Fall of the Hippest Street in the World.* London: Weidenfeld & Nicolson

Dennis, Felix (19 January 2009). *The OZ trial: John Mortimer's finest hour*. The First Post.

Devas, Nicolette (1966) *Two Flamboyant Fathers* Collins

Dolin Anton (1938) *Ballet go Round* Michael Joseph London

Dolin, Anton *Last Words* (1985) century publishing London

Duncan Robinson, E, *William Nicholson,* The Grove Dictionary of Art Online, (ed. L. Macy).

Easlea, Daryl. (2010). *Talent Is An Asset: The Story Of Sparks*. London: Omnibus Press.

Evenlyn Leith, (1945) *Ballerina,* Home & Van Thal Ltd, London

Farren, Mick, (2001) *Give the Anarchist a Cigarette*, Pimlico.

Foot, Michael, (1974), Aneurin Bevan: A Biography, Scribner, UK

Fountain, Nigel (1988). *Underground: The London Alternative Press 1966-74*, London

Gilnert, Ed. (2012). *The London Compendium: A Street-by-street Exploration of the Hidden Metropolis*. London: Penguin.

Grant M. Waters (1975). *Dictionary of British Artists Working 1900-1950*. Eastbourne Fine Art

Green, Jonathon, (1999). *All Dressed Up: The Sixties and the Counterculture.* London:

Greer, Germaine (16 July 2007). *So Emma Booth is to play me in a raunchy film about the 60s. Can't she get an honest job?* The Guardian.

Greer, Germaine, (1970), The Female Eunuch, London

Hastings, Chris, *Wings of desire: The Secret love affair that inspired Rolls-Royce's flying lady*. The Telegraph 20 April 2008

Historic England. *THE PHEASANTRY National Heritage List for England.*

Hodkinson, Mark. (2004). *Queen: The Early Years*. London: Omnibus Press

Holiday magazine, September 1951 Vol. 10, no. 3

Holroyd Michael, (1974) Augustus John Richard Clay London

Ina Taylor (1980) *The Edwardian Lady: The Story of Edith Holden,* Henry Holt and Co

Irving, Terry and Rowan Cahill, *Radical Sydney: Places, Portraits and Unruly Episodes, Sydney*: University of New South Wales Press, 2010.

Jack Kerouac, *San Francisco Blues* (1954). *74th Chorus*

Jane Elizabeth Norton (1950). *Guide to the national and provincial directories of England and Wales, excluding London, published before 1856* (1984 reprint ed.). Offices of the Royal Historical Society.

Joel, John, I paid the piper, (1970) Howard Baker London

Johnson, J., and A. Gruetzner, *Dictionary of British Artists* 1880-1940.

Joubert, Felix (1924) *Catalogue of the collection of European Arms & Armour formed at Greenock by R.L. Scott* ; v. 1, 2 and 3.

K Jackson-Barnes (2013) *The Edwardian Afterlife Diary of Emma Holden*

Kensington and Chelsea library archives

Kschessinka, Mathilde, (1960) Dancing in Petersburg the memoirs of trans Arnold Haskell, Dance books, London

Lancaster, Osbert (1956) *London Night and Day*

Levesley Richard (2011) Into My Veins AuthorHouse London

Macdonald, Nesta (1975) *Diaghilev Observed* Dance Books Ltd

Macdonald, Nesta. (1977) *The History of the Pheasantry, Chelsea, 1766–1977*. London: Nesta Macdonald

Marguerite Steen (1943) *William Nicholson, biography* Collins

Markova, Alicia, *Ballerina Known for* Giselle, *Dies at 94* The New York Times

Marsh, Jan 2015) *Art and Androgyny: The Life of Fiore de Henriquez,* The Book Mill UK

Martin Sharp, Greg Weight, *MILESAGO*. Originally published in Australian Artist.

Mester, Terri, (1997) Movement and Modernism university of Arkansas press

Michael Foot, (1962) *Aneurin Bevan: A Biography*, Faber and Faber.

Michelin. (2012*). London Green Guide Michelin 2012–2013*. London: Michelin.

Nesta Macdonald (1978) *The History of the Pheasantry*, London

Neville, Richard (1995), *Hippie Hippie Shake*, William Heinemann Australia

Nichols Robert, (1948) *William Nicholson* Penguin Books

Nichols, R, (1948) William Nicholson, Harmondsworth.

Nicholson, Andrew, (1996) *William Nicholson, Painter,* Giles de la Mare publisher Ltd London

Oxford Dictionary of Dance (2004) Oxford University Press

Oz Magazine 1967- 70

Palmer, Tony (1971*). The Trials of Oz, Blond & Briggs*.

Pendred, John (1955). *Appendix H: General Directories*. In Pollard, Graham (ed.). The Earliest Directory of the Book Trade (reprint of 1785 ed.)

Pennell, Elizabeth Robins, and Joseph Pennell, (1908) *The Life of James McNeill Whistler,* 2 vols, London and Philadelphia

Personal Correspondence with Timonthy Whidborne, Philippe Mora, Justin De Meo,

Peter J. Atkins (1990). *The directories of London, 1677-1977.* Cassell and Mansell.

Pevsner, Nikolaus & Bridget Cherry. (2002) *London 3: North West*. Reprint. New Haven: Yale University Press.

Pim, Keiron, (2016) *Jumpin' Jack Flash,* penguin random house London

Piper, David. (2000). *The Companion Guide to London* (9th revised ed.). Woodbridge: Companion Guides.

Pound, Ezra (1948) *The Pisan Cantos* New directions paperbacks ed. Richard Sieburth 2003 USA

Putterford, Mark. (2010). *Phil Lynott: The Rocker*. London: Omnibus Press.

Robertson, Geoffrey (2011*). The Justice Game*. London: Random House London

Roodhouse, Mark   (July 2005) *Nye Bevan, Black Marketeer*
History Today Volume 55 Issue 7

Ryersson and Yaccarino, Infinite Variety, The Life and Legend of the Marchesa Casati, Pimlico

Schumacher, Michael (2003) *Crossroads, The Life and Music of Eric Clapton*, Citadel Press

Sherwin, Adam (21 July 2009). *Hippie Hippie break-up as director walks*, The Times. London.

Southam, B.C. (1968) *A student's guide to the selected poems of TS Eliot*, Faber and Faber, London

Steen, Marguerite, (1943*) William Nicholson*, London.

Sutton, Tina, (2014), The Making of Markova: Diaghiliev's Baby Ballerina to Groundbreaking Icon. Pegasus Books, London

The Pheasantry Dossier, (1978) published by the Friends of the Pheasantry

The Times Archive, The Times Digital Archive 1785–1985

Thurman, Judith, *The Divine Marquise* New Yorker Magazine, September 14 2003

Tritton, Paul, (1985) *John Montagu of Beaulieu 1866- 1929* Golden eagle/ George Hart, London

V. Williams (1913). *The Development and Growth of City Directories*. Williams directory co.

Walker, Dave (2013) *The Princess at the Pheasantry*. Dave Walker, The Library Time Machine.

Woodbridge, Robinson, D, (1980), William Nicholson: Paintings, Drawings and Prints, London.

After the show at The Pheasantry with good friends: Anne Hampton Calloway, Jacqui Tate, Ann Mitchell, Sandra Holiday, Ria Jones, Richard Mowbray.

About the Author

Joanna Strand is an actress, singer, painter and print maker. She has performed in a number of opera houses, before pursuing a career in jazz and the West End.

Her recent appearances have included Phantom of the Opera, Masterclass, Bath Theatre Royal. She regularly performs jazz cabaret shows at Pizza Express, Dean Street, The Pheasantry, The Crazy Coqs, as well as New York venues including 54 Below and Birdland.

Joanna trained as a dancer at Arts Educational, and as a singer at The Royal Academy of Music. She is currently studying for a Masters in Fine Art at Central Saint Martin's specialising in print making.

The Pheasantry Today. Photo etching by the author.